trans girl suicide museum
hannah baer

for Hazel

contents

disclaimers

pt. i, symbols
early spring 2017

pt. ii, ketamine princess
late fall 2017

pt ii.5
what helped me

pt. iii
trans girl suicide museum 1: cartesian dysphoria
(can't remember when I wrote this)

pt. iv
Miami (a few days before Christmas 2017)

pt. v
trans girl suicide museum 2: just hanging out in the museum, january 14 2018

pt. vi
how to get asked your pronouns (suicide museum underwear drawer guided tour)

pt. vii
trans girl suicide museum 3: hall of mothers

pt. viii
trans girl suicide museum 4: humiliation (early spring '18)

pt. ix
trans girl suicide museum 5: neutral zone (late spring '18)

pt. x
tgsm 1000: the suicide museum refers to a specific transness, and that transness has a specific shape

afterword

references / works mentioned

disclaimers

1. What follows contains discussion of suicide, sex, death, drug use, sexual harassment, and transphobia at length.

2. My parents had fancy jobs (doctor and professor, solidly in the five percent of the wealthiest U.S. families) and I grew up with a lot of class privilege, including graduating debt-free from an ivy league school where one of my parents had tenure. So in some ways, I have little in common with many other trans people, because compared to most people in the world and even in this country, I am rich. A lot of people who are as rich as my family (e.g. "upper middle class") seem to be confused about this and don't refer to themselves as "rich," which I think is both evasive and also delusional. In particular, I think this evasion makes upper-middle-class-flavor rich people experience the delusion that class oppression (and injustice and poverty etc.) isn't their responsibility, when actually it is.

It can be really uncomfortable to talk about this – so uncomfortable in fact that most rich white people make art and say it's about ideas, or the human condition, when usually their art is also—and maybe mostly—about being rich and white. So I don't want anyone to read this and think that it was written by a universal trans girl (which doesn't exist) when in fact it was written by a trans girl who doesn't really experience the disempowerment of class oppression &/or racial oppression—and therein the specific ways that transphobia, transmisogyny, racism, and class oppression intersect. In that way this text is about richness and whiteness in addition to whatever else it's about. If for whatever reason you don't have an appetite for another artifact of wealthy white subjectivity, feel free to put this book down.

I also have a critique of identity politics or am working on one, which is a way of saying that I am hesitant to use identity categories as my primary tools for decoding all of reality. Or in other words, I don't actually feel that whiteness and wealth are the single most important things that are true about me. At the same time, I think that in order to get to a place—in our identities, and in our relationships, and in culture—where we can move past shallow or over-reliant ways of doing identity politics, people like me need to stop being evasive and delusional about our stuff.

3. I had a hope that a lot of different people would be able to read this book and feel like they basically understood what I'm talking about. Towards that goal, certain other writings that I refer to directly are included in a reference section. If you see a "**" in the text, it means you can go to the "references" at the end and see where the thing comes from.

4. I wrote a lot of this when I was thinking about certain things for the first time. The part of me that's perfectionistic wants to hide all of this beginner thinking, wants to present myself as fully formed and, well, perfected. I think especially for activists, women, and in a different but overlapping way for trans people, it can feel really shameful to be in one place in your process, and then change and be in a different place. Some of the things I wrote about below, I feel differently about now, or just more relaxed about. But I also think beginner thinking can be helpful for people to see, especially young people and trans people who are beginning, and that's partly why this book is this way.

5. A lot of people in capitalism make art and want it to be "good." I didn't write or make art in public for a long time because I think this idea of good and bad art is weird. I think it's weird to appraise or evaluate people's self-expression, to say that some people have a good or bad creativity or interiority. Accordingly, I did not try to make this book "good," and if that's what you're into, it might annoy you. I did, however, want it to be helpful to trans femme people and their friends, and I hope that it is.

pt. i, symbols: early spring 2017

I have this urge to text Lily and tell her that I have a crush on her. I have this urge to text Lily and tell her that even if she doesn't want to ever hang out with me, is it OK if I write her love letters? I have this urge to send her these love letters where I describe what my imaginative life with her is like, late night drives, sharing coconut La Croix with half a tab of acid in it and walking through the city at dawn, making out on the steps of a stranger's house, lots of eye contact during sex, a mutual insistence on a low-key relationship that feels unusually intense when we're together but then spans days or even weeks with silence and confusion, mutual obsession and moments of forgetting, making out with other people and thinking about the other, laughing about how i'm a late 20s trans girl and she's an early 20s business school student, buckets of alcohol, hours of oral sex, me talking to her about my transition.

Once I start hormones I don't know if my penis will ever get hard again. People have said things to me like "you just don't know" and "you can do it, it's just more work" but people also say things like "your penis and testicles will atrophy substantially" and "it just depends on how important erections are for your sex." I'm really not sure how important are erections for my sex. Most people who've had sex with me thought I was a man. Last week I had sex with someone, Jeannie, who I met on the internet. She wanted me to dom her and neither of us could host (i live in a basement and there's no door between my room and rest of my house) so we met in a hotel room. Before we met up I asked her via text how much small talk she wanted to have before hand, and told her it was a fantasy of mine to meet someone and just fuck them immediately, no introduction. Jeannie assented to this via text, and pressed her mouth into my mouth as soon as she walked into the hotel room. A few minutes later she was lying on her back on the bed with her head over the edge, and I was standing, fucking her throat (something she told me was her number one turn-on when we were texting) and fingering her. This isn't a way of having sex that has a particular appeal to me, but in this moment, my erection seemed pretty important. People say transgirls can take boner pills. Jeannie thought I was a man, and when I went to fuck her in the hotel room, I knew, in a way, that she was the last person I was ever going to fuck who had this deep misperception of me.

I want Lily to desire me even if my body becomes less and less like a man's body. I recently read an *Everyday Feminism* article that seemed to be criticizing the phenomenon whereby people have "genital preferences" for their sexual partners. Specifically the article was saying that it was transphobic if you were a cis lesbian who didn't want to fuck a trans girl.** It was by a trans woman who doesn't actually say outright, "cis lesbians not wanting to sleep with chicks with dicks is transphobic" but instead was instead cataloging *why* different responses (perhaps culled from YouTube comments?) to her critiques of "genital preferences" (code for 'not wanting to sleep with traps') were "problematic" (which is code for *very wrong*). Sorry if that last sentence is confusing; the whole thing was confusing for me.

I don't want to mock this person, but I did not like her article. Her general concern seemed to be that some people don't want to have sex with trans people, and her solution to that was to fashion a critique of that preference. Cyrus, who identified as a lesbian for a long time, used to say he would go on T but he was nervous about getting hairier or having his voice get deeper, but noted that he'd love to have a giant clit. So maybe I will think of my dick as a giant, floppy clit.

I don't want Lily to think it's problematic not to want to sleep with me. I don't want to feel rejected that a hot cis person doesn't want me and then make a critique of it to make myself feel better. I just want to lick Lily's vagina and asshole and put my hands inside her, and have her lick my vagina / asshole and put her hands inside me. I assume Lily is straight (I seriously barely know her) and I wonder if she'd still have texted me those different times at 10 PM asking what I was doing if she knew my dick was going to be like old chewed up gum soon, if she knew I was going to have a big floppy clit.

I lived in New York for a few years after college and then got kind of emotionally sick and had to leave. When I lived there I went on a rant once to Elizabeth about symbols. One day, fairly early on in our early romantic thing, we were in bed late at night and I was talking about not wanting to be a symbol to her. I knew from having other rich friends in New York who were invested in sub-culture and coolness that we would often describe people by describing them in symbolic categories, for example what their job was or where they went to college, rather than how they actually are in the world. Like imagine a starter pack meme, seeing the whole world like that. I had some spiritual social justice mentorship around believing that seeing people in this way was wrong, and so I believed it was wrong too. I said to Elizabeth, "I don't think of you as a hipstery art girl who lives in Bushwick, I think about what you're actually like." And I did, or I tried to anyways, I thought about her relationships with her friends and her parents, what she thought was funny and how she communicated, and how she liked to have sex, and what was off-putting to her and what she really wanted.

I also think in that moment I was being a little bit like the *Everyday Feminism* article author and feeling like it was Bad and Hurtful and Part of Capitalism for people to be invested in the symbolism of another person. I had a critique of one way people do things but the critique was actually partly coming from my pain. So with this relationship, I think I struggled, because I did recognize and make meaning out of the symbols represented by Elizabeth, that her family was rich and she had extra money to spend on clothes, and she recognized that I had fancy clothes too, and that she liked my clothes and I liked hers and we would take them off of each other and have sex with each others' pale bodies. These were part of how I experienced her and part of why we felt close to each other. Then I would also get stressed about us being too fancy, and not wanting to have that life, and I would put my stress about it on her in different ways. The critique was coming from my pain, as well as my beliefs.

I really wanted to resist seeing everything as a starter pack meme, a bundle of symbols, and I still do, to some extent. Like if someone tells me I should meet their friend, and then says that their friend is a kind of instagram-famous DJ from Greece who loves ketamine, I have trained myself to instinctively respond, even if just to myself "this is not really meaningful information about the person, except in a shallow capitalist way. I do not know if I would like them because I do not know if they are generous. I do not know if they are douche-y. I do not know if they are a grounded-and-actually-chill kind of person who ends up partying all the time. I do not know if they are addicted to visibility in a narcissistic way and if so whether I would be able to muster enough compassion around whatever their pain was in order to see them as a sympathetic character even though they might just be also really just adolescent and narcissistic and not that much fun on some deep level," etc.

I was texting Jesse recently about the difference between public and private symbols, telling him about my friend Renee.

> i tend to intensely symbolize people when i get friend crushes on them

> maybe everyone does

> but then i think one definition of shallow-ness is living in the symbol

> and not moving past it

> like right now an exciting thing to me about renee is that she's a low-key addict

> but through time i will probably just experience her more deeply as the bundle of our interactions, stilted conversations, awkward glances, and maybe our se

> x

> and the info she tells me about her

> like that her dad died last year

> or that she feels like she takes care of a lot of young people in her life

> which aren't symbols

> just things

> whereas, at least in my imagination of new york, part of how people experience each other is as symbols

> you're like "jesse the rich eccentric high school teacher"

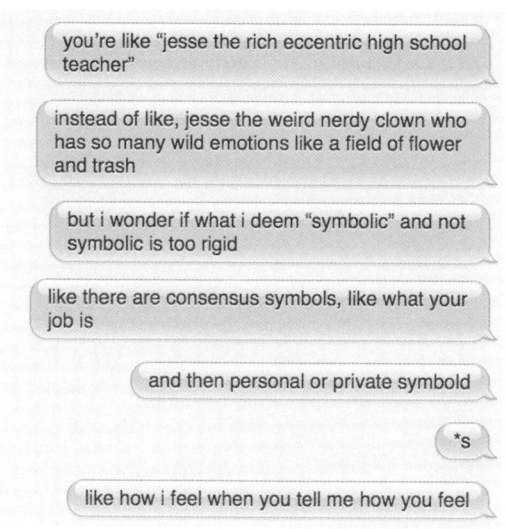

So maybe there is an arc, between when you meet someone and all you have is publicly shared symbols, like their nationality and job (e.g. "sexy boy from Greece, is a DJ") and then as you get to know them, you can deepen and enrich your understanding of who they are. Then you get the private symbols ("you were really mean to that boy after you made out with him and I wondered if it was because you feel shame around your desire") which then turn back and inflect the original shared symbols with new meaning ("part of what you're working on when you continue having a life where you're constantly traveling and constantly partying is..") etc. Or if you are a witch you get some of the private symbols first, fast data in the first impression, like, about someone's emotions or deeper qualities.

I think most of the reasons I want to sleep with Lily are from public symbols. She's young and dresses funny, she goes to business school and loves musical theater and is british and blonde and femme and she has kind of weird taste (like wearing a necklace that's just a blue glass bead, almost stoner-y, with a preppy outfit). I can't tell if what seems odd to me about her could be chalked up to her britishness. I don't know any of the things about Lily that would really let me know if she was a good friend or lover for me (like, when we texted about hanging out and she talked about going to an old-timey bar that has musical theater songs randomly performed, I had the strange feeling of knowing that I did not like things like that usually, but that I *liked her* for liking that, partly because I found it bizarre, i.e. I was invested in the symbol). I don't know how deeply she thinks about things. I don't know if she likes to have someone lick her vagina or her asshole as part of sex, or even have sex with the light on. (I had sex with another kind of normal preppy UPenn person like six or seven months ago who had some anxiety about all those things).

I don't know how Lily treats her friends, or how loyal she is, or whether she believes in healing and transformation in a deep way, I don't know if she thought I looked weird one of the first times she saw me behind the counter of the coffee shop—with a little burnt stubble on my chin from getting laser hair removal, and eyeliner and mascara on but no foundation or concealer, my shoulder-length hair in little pigtails, wearing a chunky, seethrough white sweater vest stained with coffee and a grey Calvin Klein sports bra underneath—I don't know if she would put her whole hand in my asshole. I don't even know if she thinks putting her hand in my asshole would be a normal or novel thing to do, or something she would think 'I'm the kind of person who gets all the way up to my mid-forearm in Hannah's asshole,' or if it wouldn't be part of her self-image at all. But in spite of not knowing these things, I desire her anyways. I also assume she is a cis woman, which for all I know is not the case (though I really actually think that it is the case, even though we've only run into each other in a coffee shop twice and texted for a week or something; trans people especially are not supposed to make assumptions about these things, so I'm sorry to my people, but like, she's cis).

The *Everyday Feminism* person, and I think a lot of trans liberation people, are saying "don't see penises as a symbol for man-ness, don't see vaginas as a symbol for woman-ness," and I want to do that work to not see those things as such. When my penis gets tiny and limp, like a distended belly button, it probably won't remind anyone of man-ness, maybe it will remind them of baby-ness, like a baby's dick, and maybe that will be part of my trans liberation. Maybe thinking someone's capitalist public identities are meaningful (like thinking someone is smart if they went to Wharton) is like thinking that someone's genitals are a meaningful symbol.

But I think me leaning on Lily's public symbols also has to do with what I want from her around my own trans liberation. I want a blonde british Wharton student—who believes that corporate social responsibility (rather than militant insurrection) is the best means to solve the world's most pressing problems— to also believe that my limp clit-dick-silly-putty-thing is extremely sexy. I want her to desire me even though she stands for the structures and spaces that generally don't desire trans bodies, gender non-conforming bodies. I don't care what she thinks of my insurrectionary anarchist political analysis, as long as she thinks I'm hot.

And years ago, when I lived in New York and ranted about not validating people based on symbols, I would have said that it's Bad and Wrong and False Consciousness or something, to want to be sexually and emotionally validated by a normatively hot person. But now I know it's just part of trying to make sense of my own body in oppression, and it's OK that I want Lily to desire me, and for her desire to keep me safe, in a way that's different than when hairy social justice queers desire me, because I expect it from them—because SJW queers fetishize trans women too, newsflash—and what I am actually hungry for is some kind of counter-narrative, some notion that the oppressor would deign to touch my body, sweat with my body, commune with my body, etc.

And maybe Lily desiring me won't actually liberate me all the way, maybe it will just ease the pain of this moment. Maybe wanting a normie to want to fuck you is internalized oppression, but it's also just the river I'm swimming in or the museum I'm wandering around in. Being trans, and especially a trans person who doesn't pass as a cis person (e.g. people think I'm a *really* fucked up man, or can't tell what the fuck I am) is like a symbolic 'fuck you' to people around me, for which they occasionally punish me. Symbols are part of the currency of power and we can play with them I think, but we can't simply do away with them because they are bigger than us and because they exist in and describe all of our relationships to each other and to our world.

I saw a meme recently that said it's had to say that trans women were socialized as men, that it's transphobic. I agree with parts of this and not others. I always wanted to be a woman. There are pictures of me as a kid dressed in tutus and dresses, as a toddler I loved barbies, as a pre-teen loved makeup, and have at every life phase, even in my most repressed moments, found opportunities several times a year, usually in the guise of play, to do some version of "drag." So saying I was a man before transition might be inaccurate, but saying I was "socialized" as a man—which to me means that the gender and role that other people *told me* I had/was for most of my life in most spaces was maleness (albeit effete rarified Jewish intellectual maleness)—I think is accurate, and moreover I think that this telling-of-my-gender-to-me-by-others had an impact on me. I understand the desire to refute the claim that trans women were once men (I feel shitty when people invoke my past without my consent, and people do it all the fucking time) but in some ways, my feelings about this are an appeal to queer time and private symbols, over public symbols. In public symbolism I was perceived as and treated as a man. In my private symbology, I experienced this treatment (which people call masculine socialization) and believed I *had* to be a man, I was supposed to be a man. For other trans girls, in their public and private symbolism, maybe they were never men and I respect that too. Part of the reason it's hard to generalize about these things is that—despite what cis medical students get taught at the supposedly woke SJW weekend long workshop before they misgender you at the trans clinic—trans-ness isn't one single or definitive experience.

In college when I dated Jenny and was closeted she told me that dating me was less like having a regular boyfriend and more like her relationships with her "crazy" best girl friends in high school, the ones who supported her around her eating disorder and were kind of obsessed with her and wanted to stay up all night talking. I took this as a compliment. This felt like an example of a time when someone saw me in my real gender. I *am* a "crazy" girl, and I love intense hangs with other femmes, and I love to be super-connected, and sometimes friendships with cis men feel unsatisfying—even though I *do* have special cis men friends who will stay up late with me—sometimes cis guys' capacity to really just be real and hang out and talk about emotions and experiences for hours and give each other good attention seems limited somehow. But I also don't believe that loving emotions or interconnection is an intrinsic quality of femininity (even though people do say when you start estrogen your emotions go "crazy").

Writing now, before I start hormones, I feel the feeling of "I can't wait to go "crazy," I can't wait for my mental health to become more gelatinous and my emotions to drip down my face and tits when I start estrogen," even though I have no idea what it will be like. I also feel scared of being "crazy," of the emotions being too big. Starting hormones is a symbol of transness and it's also a private experience, and it's also an expression of a will to have your private symbolism become public, like how hormones are supposed to make me grow little boobies. I want to do it, I want my little boobies to tell the world "here is a girl, that's how she feels to herself, that's the symbol she wants you to convey to her."

This discrepancy between public consensus symbols and private symbols or personal meanings is at the heart of a lot of arguments about trans shit and I don't really want to take positions on all of it because I don't know or understand everything, and I'm really so early in my process. But I do think it's weird to call out cis lesbians who don't want to have sex with trans girls on *Everyday Feminism*; it just feels off to me, like it makes me have a slimey wiggly feeling in my body, maybe because I also believe that literally no one should have to have sex with anyone they don't want to. And also I think that if there's one thing I want to critique here it's having critiques of things instead of just saying your underlying emotions, because abstract critique is part of patriarchy (and I know this because being socialized as a man for me, especially at fancy colleges, was being trained, over and over again, to hold power by criticizing things from a place of objectivity, instead of just saying my emotional intuition and not making up a reason for why it felt that way). I think because of this I sometimes feel bored when I have to deal with or engage someone's abstract critique, and it's easier and more fun for me to engage with their emotionality. In fact, sometimes abstract critiques make me angry which is why I developed an abstract critique of them.

pt. ii, ketamine princess: late fall 2017

Deep down, what is the experience of drugs, if not this: to erase limits, to reject divisions, to put away all prohibitions, and then ask oneself the question, what has become of knowledge? Do we then know something altogether other? Can we still know what we knew before the experience of drugs? Is this knowledge of before drugs still valid, or is it a new knowledge? This is a real problem and I think that in this measure the experience of drugs isn't original in our society, it's not a sort of little deviance that does not count. It seems to me that it is at the very heart of problems that the society in which we live—that is to say, in the capitalist society—is confronted with.

Michel Foucault, Interview, 1971

When I liked Lily I thought about being trans a lot. Lily called me drunk one night and told me that we should probably not hang out, even though we had never hung out and only texted (except for the two times we saw each other in the coffee shop). If I thought about being trans a lot then, now I think about it almost constantly, like a heartbreak; or I think a heartbreak is the only other thing I've thought about this much.

I am also on hormones now and I cry everyday, usually multiple times a day. I don't know if this is because I am on estrogen and T blockers or if I actually am having a specific emotional experience right now that would be different if I somehow was on the same pharmaceuticals in my body but wasn't trans, or maybe was further along being trans and less hung up on it. Is my body different than my transness? Is trans consciousness extricable from a trans body?

I get a therapist and he tries to point out ways that my bad mental health is not only related to my transition. "Bad" mental health. Trap mental health. Trap is a bad word for tranny which is a bad word for me. I'm a bad word. Is it the hormones making me like this? Only my future self will know the answer to this question but what I know now is that I'm extremely emotional, extremely distractible, and basically only interested in hanging out with my close friends. All other activities (besides taking a bath) seem kind of vague, and some activities, like sitting through a talk or a lecture or going to an activist meeting or a protest—things I used to do for fun and engagement and identity—fill my body with restlessness or even anxiety and prevent me from following through.

I've started only hanging out with other trans people, which means I just get to talk and think about being trans constantly. One question I asked my other trans friends is, if you had been assigned the other sex at birth, would you still be trans? One non-binary trans friend said that since they are not a woman or a man now, that they can't imagine identifying as either even if they had been gendered differently as a child. They thought they would be trans no matter what. Another friend, a transgirl, said she felt just so good and right as a girl, that she would definitely be cis if she was told she had been told she was a girl as a baby, child, and young adult.

One question that I would want to ask cis people is "if you were assigned the other binary gender at birth, would you transition to get back to the gender that you have now?" I don't know if very many cis people imagine this question, whether they actually experience the truth of their assigned genders so deeply that they would go through all the bullshit of transition to get back to it. If someone had asked me this when I was closeted and presenting as a cis man, I might have transitioned then and there. And that's part of what I think this question is about, namely, what happens to your consciousness if you are trans and what part of that would you recreate no matter what your assigned gender was. I want to be a girl really bad, I always have. But I also have this feeling that if I had been assigned girl at birth, I might hate it, hate sexism, and just want to be a dude. Like if a worm is reincarnated as a holy healer, they might still choose worm in the next life.

This suggestion could be very insulting to some 'binary' trans people and I get that, because I don't like when non-binary people try to be like 'gender is anything' and I'm like 'fuck you i'm a girl.' But also because the way transness has been medicalized and coded in mainstream culture makes it about flipping a switch, a corrective procedure (or set of procedures). I think about this ideology when trans girls on message boards describe themselves as pre-op or post-op, or when chasers on grinder ask me that; For me it exemplifies the extent to which people think being a transgirl is about cutting your dick off. The idea that SRS (I know that's not the politically correct name for cutting one's dick off, sry) is even a cure for the diagnosis of dysphoria reveals an extremely cis-centric framework. I'm still practicing coming out to cis people and what to say to them, but I feel like they're always wondering if I'm going to get SRS, or if i already had it. I like to tell them that I'm getting FFS, partly because I am and it's an important part of my process, and partly because I suspect like cis people won't think I'm actually trans unless they know I am getting my body cut open by a cis doctor in order to be regular.

I like having trans friends because we have similar anxieties, so we can make these special fucked up jokes. "I was on the wrong side in Auschwitz! that's my trans holocaust trauma!" I say to a trans friend whose immediate ancestors also survived the holocaust. "My mom is sad, so I guess I'm going to detransition and just go back to working at a consulting firm," I tell a friend whose mother is also having a hard time with their transition. "When people say AMAB, I just hear 'softbois on androgen-blockers,'" someone said to me recently which made me laugh a lot.

People have this other question about me being trans, which is like "did you know when you were a little kid," or something to that effect. This line of questioning is connected to the general idea that trans people feel like a [binary gender identity] trapped in a ['opposite' binary gender identity's] body. When I tell cis people that I've always wanted to be a girl, I also usually tell them that there's a lot of privilege in this narrative, because it's recognized by medical and cultural establishments as the valid trans narrative. I tell them that lots of trans people didn't have this experience but are no less trans. Cyrus, who agrees with all this stuff about normative trans narratives, recently confessed to me "I do feel I was born in the wrong body" and he was almost ashamed to admit it because we've talked so much about—and SJW trans sub-culture so enforces—how the medicalized narrative is problematic. So I also want to say that such 'conventional' trans narratives are also OK and valid, and that I wanted to be a girl when I was a little kid but that doesn't make me more trans than people who had a different experience.

One thing that did make me more trans though was ketamine. The first time I did K was with a group of friends in the summer of 2012. We railed it in thick lines and got so high we couldn't talk then stood naked on a dock in the sun by a great grey and blue lake, rolling around and on and off each others' warm bodies, like contact improv. Then we all had sex with each other.

Hazel and I hadn't spoken for almost two years when we met up in the spring of 2017 (like a month after Lily and I had stopped talking, right when I started hormones) at a restaurant in Williamsburg. She was walking with a cane because of a recent bike accident and had a bejeweled butterfly clip in her hair. We talked for a while before driving together to her apartment in Crown Heights and railing a mountain of ketamine. I saw her cutting lines on a portable digital scale and asked how much she thought was a good dose. Oh, she said, the scale isn't on.

We lay around and talked about her brothers and then she showed me this zine, *fucking trans women*, which is kind of funky, but has this whole part about the canals above the testicles, that can be penetrated, or fingered, or fucked, however you like.** We laid on our backs on her bed and fingered our pouches, staring at the ceiling and asking each other how it felt. After some practice, I could put my index finger all the way under my skin, from where my scrotum starts all the way to the top of my pubic hair. I felt like an alien. How did you find K, I asked Hazel? I was trying not to commit suicide, she said.

The rest of that summer it was like that, as Hazel would say, it was really like that. We spent a week in Truro floating from beach to movie theater to fireplace everywhere cutting up ketamine on mirrors, cellphones, book covers. One night we got high and I put makeup on Hazel, she hadn't been wearing it much. My hand holding the liquid eyeliner pen was like an obelisk, a magic wand, sliding with glacial slowness a mark across her delicate lash line. I applied blush to her cheekbones, I smushed lipstick into the crevices of her lips. We stared at her in the mirror. I can't believe what I look like, she said. I can't believe that we exist, I said. That fall we got matching tattoos of razor blades with each others names on them on our arms because we are sisters and also traps and also because we love doing k.

I want to try to say more clearly what ketamine means to me. One time I went to a party in the late fall of 2017, in Philly, in a warehouse that had been converted into big apartments. Lincoln and I drove there and did key bumps of k in the car parked outside. We were ushered in (someone had gotten us onto the list I think) and there was a dancefloor and makeshift bar and some lights, and I didn't know what else to do besides more k. Lena was there and we were in our thing, and that was also the night I met Beth, who I partied with all the time in the weeks and months after that, and also I met this person Amy who I thought was a transgirl but actually just had an incredibly square jaw and deep voice.

Amy said we should do Calvin Klein, CK, which is cocaine and ketamine at the same time. We were in the stairwell of the warehouse and I agreed. It felt so good. I felt waves rippling through my body. This feels so good, I say. Amy, in her low monotone, tells me: that's why the brand Calvin Klein is so popular. There was an open window in the stairwell and it was extremely cold so I needed to go back into the party and we went in and suddenly I couldn't stand up and thought I was going to puke. I sat down on a couch too close to a stranger, in that way you only do at a party if you're fucked up and just need to sit down before you fall down. I was just trying to chill and Lincoln brought me some water and I breathed a lot.

I suddenly turned to look at the stranger next to me and realized she was a beautiful trans femme, dressed like a cat, by which I mean that they had on a fuzzy hood with cat ears on it and whiskers drawn on their face. (re-reading this later I realize it's problematic to "know" that someone is trans femme by just seeing them, partly because you're not supposed to know people's gender without asking and partly because of politics of passing stuff; but i hope that, especially for well-meaing cis people reading this, you can just hold the contradiction and feel the wonder of two trans femme people non-verbally recognizing each other). We introduced ourselves to each other and they asked how I was doing. I explained that I had done coke and K at the same time and that I felt a little sick. The room was loud and quiet at the same time, dark except lasers, the couch felt like a giant squishy mouth. My interlocutor's face dropped: "you have K?" Yeah, I said, you want some. I could barely move. She explained that she was a drug dealer and began to tell me all the different drugs she had on her person that she was able to trade for K. It's OK I said, you can just have some, I said, I probably can't do more drugs right now I feel sick. She used a tiny spoon she wore around her neck to snort the powder that I was carrying in a little glass tub that used to hold the hippie deodorant that Elizabeth bought for me.

Look, said my new friend on the couch. Sitting across from us, in the loft, in the middle of the party, perched atop a giant subwoofer, was a white and orange cat, seemingly relaxed despite the pounding music and the dozens of people. Looking at the cat, she said: "I identify as feline." To be clear, k is not hallucinogenic in this way– there really was just a cat at the party, gazing at us from atop the speaker. In this moment I felt in my body some deep truth about ketamine and transness, watching this feline trans person do my drugs on this couch with this cat, I really felt her girlness, I really experienced her and my own transness. I want to explain it more but it's hard.

My friend Eli did K with me and said he felt like he was able to intensely compartmentalize on K so maybe that's part of it. Sometimes trans people's gender presentations or experiences can have these different dissonant parts in them and k gives me the liberated compartmentalized eye to just see the ones they want me to see. In my own body too, when I'm on the drug, I feel my own transness, my own capacity for pleasure, my own deep bitch woman cunt femme sassy sister girlness, my angelness, my sweet baby bitchness, all that is tender and beautiful in my fucked up body. The ways when sober I sometimes feel like a gross boy, a big white whale body with a deep sonorous voice and gigantic cock, all fades on K, so when I am high on the white crystals I am like a floating light white bitch, a little girl angel, a delicate glass femme slut. Or, in different words, it helps me with the cluster of symptoms that cis doctors have agreed to call dysphoria.

OK OK i just did a bunch more K to try and tell you about this.

one thing is that K makes me more like moses (moses was a trap maybe) because it makes me lose my words, and moses was supposed to be bad at talking (that's why aaron had to go with her to chill with pharaoh).** I'm so voluble normally (see even when really hi i write words like voluble) but when I'm on K my language stuff chills my anxiety chills, everything just cools right fuck off. No neon colors, just greys, blues, some muted pastels. maybe somewhere between pastels and earth tones. The spectrum of blue light that comes from the iPhone screen, that's ketamine

sometimes K feels like something is squeezing my brain, extruding it through a plastic pussy, i want to say star-shaped to be funny but that's not what it feels like, it's kind of like just pressure i guess, the extrusion doesn't actually happen. you are just there, at the meniscus (i mouth this word as I type it) suspended, and that is what is brilliant about k, the feeling of suspension, the feeling of time completely dilating, a single song lasts for sooooo longg-ggggg, you can go so fast when everything seems so slow, and words just come out and out and out. (if you've ever done poppers it can kind of be like that but extended?)

but that's the thing about losing my words, like, i'm so verbal and k helps me chill. it's also like a test though, like a gauntlet of verbal ideation, like, can you get extremely high and still have a really fierce conversation; When i did k with rebecca the therapist we could just keep talking the whole time - - - and we just kept talking and talking, like being able to sprint in a weighted vest, neurons still firing even though the glassy crystals were slicing the pathways. i guess it's like a friendship trial, can you still keep up a really good convo with me when you're blunted on k, that is good for me. one time Cyrus and I did K off of an expensive piece of art in his parent's house and talked about saints and angels and how we couldn't do coke anymore, only k, because being fast on coke feels bad but fast on K feels like being a spirit floating free above the world, out of the body, which is also one reason I think trans people i know like K.

When I'm really hi on k my eyes don't totally focus and I become uncoordinated. Unlike the sloppiness of alcohol, however, I can feel the slur, if i tune into it, i I can feel the muscle memory working to keep my limbs and digits moving, feel the muscles in my legs twitching to keep my unwieldy trap frame upright, even as I sway and swirl, i can watch myself do what i do, watch and feel my body, it's the most cinematic thing in the world. Which is important for being trans, to be able to watch yourself, to feel your body differently. Do you get it. k makes me so aware of my body in certain selective ways, if and only if i choose to put my attention on it. Hazel said she likes to do alexander technique on it.

hazel and i went to go see the new jumanji on k and screamed in the theater because for much of the movie jack black is playing a teenage girl, just being fully trans, and it's so beautiful. we did more and more k in the theater, watching her talk about how she didn't know how to pee standing up, how she didn't understand what the thing was between her legs, listening to her trans voice. Jumanji was maybe the most trans-affirming movie, though it probably was problematic too and i just didn't get it bc i was too high ,,,

there's this idea in philosophy in the last 60 years that the category of a person (or "a subject") is actually socially constructed, rather than natural and/or handed down from g-d. The idea is something like "what if this category of 'person,' along with all its supposedly 'natural' elements (gender, erotic desire, emotions, intelligence, etc.) is actually produced by culture rather than nature?" I believed this idea—that the 'natural subject' was not natural—for a long time but I wasn't sure what it meant, like practically, to believe this idea if you had been told you were a 'natural'—rather than a cultural—subject your whole life. And especially if you lived in a world where everything from deodorant commercials to the supreme court believe people are natural subjects, with DNA that tells the truth of our bodies and higher consciousness that justifies us killing animals, etc.. basically what i'm saying: the category of person is a myth, but, like gender, a myth we are trapped in..

the thing is, sometimes i feel like less of a subject on K. it's hard (or stupid?)_ to even try and use language to say it because part of how the natural subject comes to us is in language (like "I" have to speak in words and choose whether or not iiii capitalize the letter 'i') but I want to try and say it: somehow, it's like these cultural instructions which say 'my perceptions make me into an individual' are suddenly inactive and I can just perceive without being, or without being necessarily meaning that I am a human person with a name and socio-cultural laws and an assigned gender and a gendered history et cetera. This feeling of being not one single person, of being dialed in to just-experience, with no self, can also feel transcendent, though without any of the pomp or pretense that that word carries. Just like in a literal way, my body is not the walls and my mind is not the story of me and my sex is not my truth, I'm just like all these things, all these girls, all these trans girls through history, all these Jewish girls through history, all these closeted trans people with horrible secrets, all these little kids getting in trouble for playing in the wrong way, I feel myself inside of and reflecting back a legacy. maybe this is why it feels like the internet. I want to name this manuscript "Herculine Barbin high on ketamine on a stranger's couch in Tampa or San Diego reading about herself on a .pdf on her cracked iphone with five percent battery left and no charger"**

Another thing about K is it feels so connected to the internet. I can't imagine being trans without the internet. If you are holding this book in your hands, I hope you are high on k and I hope you are on the internet. The way I can think on k is like drop-down menus in an interface that reads HTML and CSS at the same time, consciousness without an individual subjectivity is like websites.

One time Hazel rented a convertible for us to drive around in and we did our favorite game where one of us gets really high and the other one stays sober and drives us. We were on the highway and I was so high in the convertible, talking about the walls of the car, and how the car is like one space but it's actually not discrete, because if I lift something and let it go, it floats away. I picked up a receipt from the floor of the car and lifted it between me and hazel's faces and let it go: it was gone. I did it again with a bottle cap and with a hair tie. Look, I said, the space is not discrete, there is no boundary between here and there, inside and outside. Hannah, hazel said, you're just throwing trash out the car.

It's weird being on k and thinking about the morality of drugs, how k is a rarified way to get high, that the people who culture appoints as its arbiters of morality somehow have decided that this way to have fun is more fucked up than other ways to have fun, thinking about people watching TV, scrolling through instagram, looking at pornography, getting blackout drunk, wandering around shopping malls. It's good to do all those things, I think, but it's more fun on k. I must also say that part of what makes k so perfect is its illegality, its weirdness, the way it's treated in culture. I think it would be less fun to do k if you could buy it at CVS, no doubt. but I don't think this means the way i do it is any less meaningful. I think if you could buy k at CVS and getting alcohol required me to sit in my car and do active listening to a shy, closeted 23-year-old while he talked to me about his relationship with his family before he sold me the drug then maybe I would be writing about how whiskey changed me right now.

but whiskey makes me feel sick because i'm on t-blockers.. oops

I sometimes worry that I can't hold enough complexity on k, that it oversimplifies my thinking, reduces everything down to these chunky crystals that get sliced by a razorblade and scraped by the enormous edge of a dollar bill before floating up into my nose and beading into the moisture on the end of a nose hair (consciousness)

But I know that k taught me what Foucault said about drugs to be true, and also what Jesse and I used to refer to "The Bill Vollman thing" referring to the idea that this guy Bill Vollman had allegedly once said that the point of doing drugs was to be able to recreate the same experience when you're not on drugs (seriously, the last time I thought about "the Bill Vollman thing" was probably 2013) but I think the 'vollman thing' was right; k actually did change me and if before I doubted my gendered experience, I now don't have any doubt about it—I know I'm a trap now because I did this drug, it warped my reality and even when I'm not on it, i'm still a girl.

One thing Hazel and I talk about about k is that when you're really high on it, it's hard to ever remember not being on k, like you go back re-write your conscious experiences as those of a high person, or you can't recall them at all. This retroactive warp, coupled with amnesia, weirdly mirrors some moments of transness. It's hard to remember exactly what it was like when I just felt comfortable in public, like maybe I never actually did. But I think I must have. But I can't totally reach it anymore, it's blurred by the transgirl ketamine halo. I'm just me now.

I tell my friends via email the date of my facial feminization surgery. I'm crying because I'm so happy. It's the afternoon and I'm alone in a tiny house in someone's backyard in a suburb in south florida. I do these big lines of k and float. Cyrus writes back that he's waiting to hear about his top surgery date, which is around the same time. I write back: "I wish we could get cut open next to each other like a couples massage" ;; this is my brain on k

pt ii.5, what helped me

Besides doing k every day I had some really significant experiences between when I started identifying as non-binary and using they/them pronouns and when I started to ID as a full trap. I went to visit Cyrus in Los Angeles in the fall of 2016, after we had had a rest in our friendship for a year or so. He was excited to see me because he had heard from a mutual friend (maybe Carolyn?) that I was messing with my gender and he had strong feelings about my gender.

Cyrus was one of the first people to tell me that I wasn't a boy. One time after we had led a social justice retreat together in the summer of 2014 we were laying on the floor in the back room of Hazel's parents labyrinthine farmhouse in rural Vermont. I remember lying on the floor in just sweatpants and a pink American Apparel sports bra and telling him how I hated being read as a man at the helm of the retreat. You don't have to do it, he said, you don't have to be a man. I do, I said, I have this privilege and I need to use it. You don't need to do it he said. I need to do it I said, it's the ethics of being a man, I have to use my privilege (this is what I had been taught by one of my social justice mentors).

We went outside to spend time with the other people who worked on the social justice retreat, all of whom identified as cis at the time (though in the years that followed, like half our staff of 8 transitioned, many of us out of touch with each other in the times that our transitions were starting). One of the boys, someone I'd known since I was a young teenager, almost scoffed and asked, are you wearing a bra. We had just spent 8 days in the woods with thirty 20-24-year-olds talking about oppression and power and I had been the effective leader. Certain things were expected from me and other things were not permissible. I knew this feeling because it had happened periodically throughout my life, usually once or twice a year when I did full drag or even just put on lipstick or had my nails done or some other visible femme marker. I would do it in public and someone, usually a man that was my friend, would react, usually in a negative way.

I pin this feeling to a memorable morning during my first month of eighth grade when my gentle Marxist father was enraged to see me going to school wearing a bra. I had just shaved my head—I had a kind of a shoulder-length feather cut dyed emerald green just before that—and I think wanted to look more femme. I remember wearing a tight white athletic shirt over a white bra that a friend from summer camp had given me. I stuffed the bra with toilet paper. I wore a long black flowing skirt, that I maybe had found in my sister's closet. My father had this specific brooding look that I recognized from getting in trouble as a kid. Almost like he was shaking but his body was still, like the wavelengths of his energy suddenly got too tight. What are you doing, he asked. He was furious and I could feel it. I went to school in my outfit anyways, outwardly defiant, yet also—as with most times I got in trouble as a kid—inwardly scared that I would lose his love. Halfway through the school day that day I was called into the guidance counselor's office. The guidance counselor informed me that someone had complained that I was making fun of girls who stuff their bras and that I needed to go into the bathroom and take off the bra. Maybe I had made a joke about girls stuffing their bras, though I couldn't remember having done so, that day or as I write this now. I was thirteen and did not know the word 'transmisogyny' so I took off the bra.

Before I went to visit Cyrus in the fall of 2016 I had spent over a year thinking and talking about my transness in delicate and tentative ways, asking only my closest friends to use 'they' pronouns for me, secretly buying beautiful dresses that I was afraid to wear, covertly putting on bras in dressing rooms and staring at myself as I wept. But I decided that when I went on this trip to LA, I was going to push it a notch further. I only packed dresses, and brought lots of razors, planning to maintain a hairless face and body for the whole trip.

The trip and the experience of being trans identified everywhere I went melted my face off. Cyrus had somehow made an itinerary for us that involved socializing with almost only trans women. We went to a protest about low pay at the LGBTQ center in Hollywood led by transwomen, we went to a trans night at a gay club, we drove a girl to her court date for an arrest related to her political organizing. One night we had dinner with Ashley, a colleague of Cyrus's (at a restaurant in Rosemead called JTYH Heavy Noodle, where the noodles are thick and slimy and endless, like the genitals of trans people, and also so delicious).

Ashley, maybe because she was white and I am white, or maybe because she was closer with Cyrus than other people I met that week, or maybe just because she was able to do compelling self-disclosure openly and with minimal prompting, told me everything about her process. She told me about hormones, about experiencing her emotions and queerness newly on hormones. She talked about how she felt about her body, her boobs and her face, and when she passed and when she didn't. I asked her about SRS. "I love my dick" she said. And then added "some chicks have dicks." No one had ever said this to me so clearly before and I suddenly felt that someone had told me an incredible truth, one I wanted to repeat loudly to strangers and spray paint on walls: The inevitable telos of transfemininity was not castration.

I actually kind of had secretly wanted SRS all my life, from when I read a queer children's book *The Boy Who Wanted a Baby*** at age 7 or 8, (no idea how my parents gave me this book and then were mad that I transitioned but go figure) to when I was 13 or 14 and read *Trans-Sister Radio*** , an Oprah's-book-club-kind-of novel by a cis guy that meticulously details an adult woman's transition and her surgery. But I wasn't ready to really go there in my head and heart in this palpable moment of transness. I had heard all the rhetoric about genital essentialism, but I just actually hadn't gotten to hang hard with a trans girl before, and even though I didn't believe that my penis was keeping me a boy, some part of me also did. So when Ashley told me I could still be a girl and have a penis, that it wasn't an either/or, and really, hearing her say it about herself, that she was really a girl and loved her penis, it felt like a green light.

I didn't know how crazy I would go when I started, and I didn't know how much less I would care about my penis, and I didn't understand all the things that would happen to my body. But I immediately got on the computer at home and started researching hormones.

Hazel says being trans is like an STI, you get it from other people. I think this can be true and I also think anyone could have been Ashley for me that night, I was looking for people to tell me to go forward. That's why it's confusing to talk about whether transition is a choice– because once I started listening to myself and searching, I didn't feel like I was choosing anymore.

There is a whole tapestry of moments like this one with Ashley that I have tried to catalog in different ways at different times, catalytic moments when I felt like I could get closer to being a girl, like my girlness was real or valid, when I believed that it was OK not just to *want* to be a girl but to actually *be* a girl. My original tapestry list was chronological but eventually the framework of specific meaningful moments of trans insight or inspiration became irrelevant as I actually started to get into the museum of my own transness. It was no longer an aberration to have an insight about my transness, or a conversation about it. It became the only insight, the only kind of conversation. Some chicks have dicks, Ashley told me, but she didn't also tell me that some chicks with dicks go psycho.

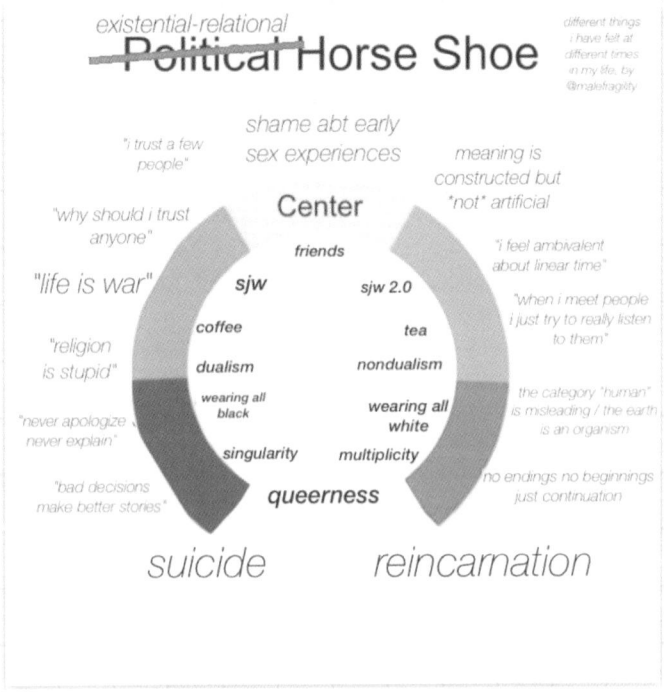

[this meme is about getting out of the suicide museum]

pt. iii, trans girl suicide museum 1: cartesian dysphoria (can't remember when I wrote this)

I told Claudia the name of this manuscript. Claudia said there was a thing on tumblr that was like 'define your gender in five words' and she said my five could be trans girl suicide museum, even though it's only four. Claudia also told me a very helpful analysis of what suicide is, which I will share here, in part because I wrote any of this shit down hoping myself not to die by my own hand, and for no other trans girls (and no trans guys, and no non binary people, agender people, or anyone else who has deviant gender and does suicide) to feel that they have to die in order to get through it, and I think Claudia's analysis helped me. She said suicide is what happens when one's internal and external life context overwhelms one's resources to keep living. It helped me to think of suicide like this as a kind of tipping mechanism, a result of overwhelm. In a healing/transformation framework, suicide can be prevented by changing a person's life context or by fortifying their inner resources to tolerate the horror of being alive.

When my friend called me a month ago saying that they were thinking about ending it, I imagined us together squatting on the low end of the seesaw, feet in leather stirrups fastened to the floor with big metal bolts, making sure we stayed down. I was behind her with my arms around her waist like a motorcycle passenger, while hundreds of things fell on the upper side of the seesaw, pouring down, trying to tip it: their parents, their dead ancestors, the surgeon that performed gender affirming surgery on them, hundreds of pounds of trash, especially *bad* trash, like dirty diapers, hypodermic needles for hormones, hypodermic needles for dope, dog shit bags that ripped open, mice traps with dead mice in them (can mice be trans) and of course hundreds of gallons of menstrual fluid, semen, crude oil, spit, diarrhea, malta goya, iced coffee, the restaurant grease traps that trans people clean because they can't get other jobs—really just anything that goes down a drain—raining down trying to tip the seesaw. I don't know why there's malta goya except my friend who tried to get me to kiss his penis when I was five years old loved malta goya. I'm scared to include this last sentence because I know some people believe that transpeople are only trans because of childhood sexual experiences that they could heal from and then be cis. Hazel started making a film collage of all tropes about transwomen from mainstream American movies, and found that a recurrent trope, especially from thrillers and horror movies, was that we are crazy traps because bad stuff happened to us when we were kids, and that is what made us psychos or murderers in the movies, which is ironic because we are more likely to be murdered than other people, especially if we are black or brown, and we are more likely to murder ourselves. We are more likely to cling to the floor while the trash pile streams down on the high end of the seesaw, we are more likely to be flung into space, sucked up into the trash chute, and gone.

The trans girl suicide museum isn't necessarily a place you go in order to kill yourself, much in the way that people don't necessarily go into an art museum in order to do art. There is definitely a room in the museum with the seesaw in it, or at least there is in my museum. Imagine the most normal white sterile high-ceilinged art gallery room you can picture, and then imagine a yellow metal seesaw in the middle of the room, with a giant opening over the high end of it, a mechanical cisgendered vagina ready to dump transphobia on you and lift you, from your seat on the low-end, up into quiet. But it's not just that. It's as much spending the hours between 3 and 5am scrolling-through-old-pictures-on-your-external-hard-drive-looking-at-your-bone-structure-from-when-you-were-a-kid-and-teenager as it is suicidal ideation.

In the horror movie *Oculus* there's a haunted mirror that two siblings are trying to destroy, because the mirror makes people do bad things. One sibling builds a giant metal spike on a pendulum, hitched to the ceiling, prepared to swing down and smash the mirror. But in the final moment when the pendulum comes down, the girl sibling who built the whole device is somehow standing in the way– the mirror protects itself, and she is murdered, penetrated by her own pendulum spike, guts spilling out onto the floor in front of the haunted mirror. Part of gazing at one's self in transphobia (and perhaps in hyper-capitalist individualism consumerism in general) is the myth that looking at yourself heals you, when it might in fact be haunting you, poisoning you, tricking you into disemboweling yourself.

ARE TRAPS TRAPPED IN THE MUSEUM? idk. the texture varies so much based on money. the trans people I know who have some level of class privilege get to stay in the museum in a particular way, like I know someone who has EBT and a parent co-signed credit card, someone who works minimum wage only two-days a week, lots of people depending on random monetary kickbacks from family members or other kinds leaked down accumulated capital (getting gifted a car, getting to stay in a second home, getting little gigs from one's parents or their friends, not having debt from school etc.) Girls I know who don't have family money do sex work, work weed, sell drugs, have sugar daddies, are transient, are strategizing. Some girls with loaded families lose access when they transition. Most girls I know, regardless of class, can't work normal office jobs and wouldn't want to if we could. Some girls I know have learned to code because you can work remotely and never have to go into an institutional building with normal people. The things you can do to scrape by, the sources from which you draw strength, the things cisheteropatriarchy permits you to do, the limits of what you can tolerate.** Your imagination inside the walls wondering if the walls themselves can move.

I feel trapped in the museum right now and part of what that means for me is that I have very little attention for anything not related to transness, my own or other people's, but almost unlimited attention for transness, like maybe the way evangelical christians feel about Jesus or like how a drowning person feels about air.

One thing I also don't know is if traps actually ever leave the museum. I think I've kind of been in it since an acid trip in the winter of early 2017 when I pounded the floor of my room and wept at 8am thinking about how oppression is fundamentally about being close to death (in part because I had been reading this writing about AIDS and Act Up by Pippi Kessler and how activists are close to death)** after spending many hours at the DJ set of some chicago house person (where I took the acid) and dancing until my friend got too stressed about how it was hard to dance because people kept walking through the dancefloor, and also he was tripping, so we went back to his house with his partner (we were all tripping hard) and listened to Tinariwen and he asked me about if my family had money or not (his family had money). At 7am that morning I took a lyft the three quarters of a mile back to the basement room where I lived then and at 8:30 or so I texted the person I was dating at the time, M, and asked them to come over before work because I couldn't sleep or stop crying, and they did come over for a minute and were nice to me; in the basement room I had pinned a bath towel over the garden-level window in my attempt to sleep at 8 in the morning, and the low winter sun was blasting through the window; the way the towel fell, there was a tiny aperture in the folds of fabric through which a piercing shard of light came through, causing a blinding cadmium diamond to land directly on—and fully illuminate—my pillow. I thought it was extremely funny because I really wanted to sleep, but was too hot to keep my head under the covers (because I was still tripping and couldn't stop sweating) and yet when I took my head out to look around, I was blinded by this razor sharp spotlight and couldn't possibly fall asleep. M thought it was funny too and offered to adjust the towel for me and they were giving me care in this specific way that I have now learned I really wanted in that part of the museum, and anyways that is the morning I think I entered the museum, because when I was crying, I was crying about how I couldn't be an activist right now, about how I just have to be doing something extremely fierce and internal, and I didn't know when it would end. I met Lily shortly after this. If this was a more literary or more pretentious piece of writing I would probably try to connect this particular experience at this particular time to the 2016 election, but I don't feel like it X_x

So, as I said before, one thing I also don't know is if traps actually ever leave the museum, like if I will be a weepy introspective bitch when I'm 50, taking my straight friends' kids out to the movies and silently crying about cis-normative messaging in the film, or about which bathroom to use, or the way the teenage movie theater cashier looks at my gigantic tits that maybe I will have when I'm 50 because literally who the fuck knows. I met this girl recently and we were talking about the museum (I think I described it as being really focused on myself and my transness in this phase of my transition) and I was saying I felt like it was going on and on in this phase, and she said totally she knew exactly what I was talking about and I asked how long she felt like she had been in it, and she said like five years and I realized that it might go on forever for me too, even as I write this, that acid trip day was like 11 months ago, and i'm not sure if that is a short time or a long time.

I don't usually describe my experience as being trapped in a boy's body because my body has always felt like a faggot bitch body, from my bony hips and skinny waist to my long muscular legs and tight asshole. My roommate in boarding school once saw me lying in bed in a pair of tight briefs and said I had a girl butt. No matter what I tried in my cis guy life, real guys always thought i was a little bitch. it makes more sense to describe it as being trapped in a museum because my body belongs to me and i love it, but the thing I'm trapped in someone else built and i can't find the door.

Before I started trying hard to pass, I felt OK about how I looked. It wasn't until I realized that my protruding brow bone or big hands were a giveaway that I started to feel that they were disgusting. I think I was so happy when I started to look more femme that it took me a minute to figure out I still was being read as a man, an unhappy reality I was made aware of by stares from strangers, but that I fully felt, randomly one day, early into my public transition when I was staring at a picture of myself on instagram, one of the first outwardly gender variant-looking pictures I'd posted. It was a tired early-morning make-up smeared selfie, just my face, standing outside some DC pizza restaurant that had been in the news during the fall of 2016 (ok ok it was comet ping pong, google it), having come from M's parent's house shortly after dawn. When I posted it I felt almost giddy—I thought I looked so femme. But after some more time passed, maybe another six months, I saw the picture and saw what probably most others saw: a boy with a girlish haircut, girlish eyebrows, and no facial hair, with mascara smudges under his eyes.

Even after this revelation though, this lens shift, I still don't like hating my body. I'm on hormones now so my breasts are coming in and they're beautiful and I love them, but I didn't dislike my pecs before. Now sometimes I wish my breasts were bigger, or that my chest looked like some conventional/normative idea of a girl chest and not a boy chest, but I also never disliked my pecs. It's funny to write this because I wanted to be a girl for so long and I think repressed it in part because I was afraid of being a freak or getting in trouble or getting beat up (or other things that were palpable threats when I was a young girl). I think part of the medicalized cis narrative of transness is about there being a *problem* with a given body, necessitating an intervention that medical professionals can deem appropriate and administer. Even though I know I repressed my transness, I'm not sure I repressed hating my body, I might have actually just felt loving towards my body.

And while dysphoria is a real experience for a lot of people, it's also focused on pathology and negation, on getting rid of assigned gender. It's nice for me to think about transness not as just a getting-rid-of, but as a manifesting, an imagining, an inception, an integration. Dysphoria, as a pathology, being the requisite marker of transness, connects to the idea that trans people should want to be cis people. Trans people can want to be whatever they want, but sometimes when trans girls really want to be cis girls, it reminds me of my Jewish ancestors, really wanting to be white Americans, but not being able to get rid of their slavic accents or semitic bone structure. I want to be a cis woman, but I'll never be a cis woman, I'll always be a trap, no matter how many surgical vaginas I get sewed into my body. If you think this invocation of my Jewish ancestors is somehow anti-surgery, just know that I'm so excited to get FFS I can't fucking wait. When Hazel said she was scared of getting FFS because they would want to rhinoplasty her Jewish nose to make it look goyish, I told her she was joining a long legacy of Jewish women who had gotten plastic surgery on their noses. I was re-reading this last sentence, almost comatose from k, just getting out of a lyft and stumbling into my bed, thinking about the idea of being part of a long legacy of jews, a long legacy of traps, a long legacy of crazy people. I can't decide if I should take off my baby blue Issey Miyake pants that Elizabeth bought me on my birthday in 2015 or sleep in them like they are pajama pants. I feel ashamed to wear them out in West Philadelphia because they are too fancy. I write a note on my iPhone: i am part of a long legacy of transgender jewish women living in west Philadelphia and coming home high on k wondering if i should take off my issey pants before bed.

Another weird thing about dysphoria is that it's treated as a problem between the mentally ill trans' person's brain and their supposedly healthy body. This is why my second wave feminist cis mother is scared that I want to get facial feminization surgery: because my body is healthy and doesn't need to get chopped up. Only a sick-mind would want to chop up a healthy-body. I think of this understanding of dysphoria—a taut relationship between an isolated individual's brain and an isolated individual's body—as a kind of cartesian dysphoria, by which I mean a dysphoria that deeply depends on the difference between the body and the mind, and treats individuals as isolated and self-governing, mental illness and all.

Regular trans affirmation then is cartesian both because it depends on a body/mind split, and because it is linear, it maps onto a cartesian plane, with time on the X axis and true transness on the Y axis. At some point you cross a threshold of transition, and you finally *are* trans, maybe when you get your genitals cut up, or maybe when you finally pass all the time, or when a hot-cis-person-who's-not-woke-about-gender (like Lily) wants to fuck you and thinks your gender is real and normal and hot. If this last one is the marker, maybe no one ever gets to be really trans.

My experience of dysphoria—and really my experience of gender altogether— is best described by something Cyrus first talked about with me, namely the idea that your gender is not something you experience only in isolation, but something that is reflected back to you by other people, that gender is what leaks out in the eyes of cis people clocking us in public bathrooms or our family members making assumptions about us, and the ways the leakage bounces back and ricochets and echoes—in dressing rooms and the lines at nightclubs, and at airport security and in the line at Walgreens when you look like a girl and you're buying condoms and enemas—and then also that is held up or shone upon us by other queer people, by our trans sisters and siblings, by other gender variant friends and familiars.

Gender flickers, hiccups, and spins. It creeps and it slithers, it infects and it disappears. Not being trapped in a body, being trapped in a museum. If, as Cyrus said, one's gender is something partially constituted by the gender that people reflect back to you, then part of being trans for me is *deciding* to make a claim on the gender I want reflected back to me, instead of just letting people reflect it back to me as they wanted. I'm thinking about one of the people who taught me a lot about social justice when I was younger telling me it was wrong for me, supposedly a "man," to want to be a woman, and I at the time, accepted what was being reflected back. The dissonance of other people reflecting back to me a gender that's different than the one I am claiming—the one I'm giving myself permission to experience, the one I'm melting into—is one definition of transphobia, this dissonance and all the violence that comes with it. The first and most important ongoing part of my transition has been being in community with other queer and trans people, and so if you are thinking you might want to reclaim or re-narrate the gender that people reflect back to you, my advice is to try and hang out with other queers. And also if someone tries to talk to you about your transness by asking what gender you would have on a desert island, you can tell them you wouldn't have a gender in the same way because gender is inextricably relational, not merely individual.

Me and Cyrus and our other friends didn't invent the idea that gender is unstable, and I imagine that people felt it in some way even before it was 'invented' as an idea, though such imagining gets a little tricky. This doctor and historian Jonathan Metzl says that it doesn't make sense to talk about schizophrenia in, say, the 15th century, because the cultural category did not exist yet.** Even if people were doing a comparable set of behaviors that today we would identify as schizophrenic, the legal, social, and biological frameworks implicit in the category of schizophrenia and so the thing we talk about today, in all of our current versions, did not exist. Like, if you live in a communal culture where everyone believes in God and thinks everything is connected to God and the community, then hearing voices is a fundamentally different thing than in an individualist scientific-secular culture like the one I grew up in (people have studied this difference too). Our categories don't move across history and culture cleanly, Metzl is saying. So it's responsible, if we're looking at a medical category (including transness) to look at its history and culture. Probably there are people studying this, but because I'm just a party girl and not a scholar I actually don't know what the most up-to-date people are saying. Maybe some day when I do less drugs or have sex with fewer people I will wake up early and go running and then make a helpful reading list for you of trans people writing about the social-historical construction of transness.

There's this other thing Foucault says, which I think is related, he says that homosexuality was invented in the nineteenth century.** This idea is important to me in trying to understand my experience. What he's talking about, I think, is that there were men who fucked other men and women who fucked other women all through history, but it wasn't until the 19th century that we called these people "homosexual" and put them in that category, which has a specific set of legal, social, and biological implications, including that their behavior was now pulled into the spider's web of shared cultural recognition, even if just as a deviant identity. There's all kinds of examples of this, but how an average person experiences living after the invention of homosexuality could be demonstrated by stereotypes of gayness. Cultural familiarity with gay stereotypes (cis men, promiscuity, circuit parties, and HIV) are not because that's what gayness is or what gay experience is, but because that's how the category was constructed in order to uphold myths about straightness, purity, and monogamy. In other words (and this also from Foucault) homosexuality wasn't invented in order to give gay people better healthcare or more respectful employers, it was invented (perhaps analogously to the way Columbus "discovered" the American continent) in order to increase the reach of power, to map out, identify, taxonomize, and regulate what exists, what is known, what can be.

This idea, that these categories are historically and culturally dependent, is important to me.

One reason it's important to me is because we are in the century-long process of the categorical invention of the trans woman. Hannah Arendt wrote (I actually can't remember where or I would cite it, maybe somewhere in *Between Past and Future*) that it was fundamentally different to be a Jewish person before the foundation of the state of Israel. She didn't mean better or worse, more fucked up or more liberated, but just that there was a shift in consciousness for people with this identity around this historical event. And I wonder about this with transness, what was it like to be a transgirl in the 50s, or the 1850s, and how did girls then feel and act, how did they relate to their bodies, how did they think about ideas we have now like passing or dysphoria. Did they feel like girls, or like women, or like ghosts, or like some other thing I wouldn't think of off the top of my head because I live in a particular historical time, such that my parents rented the *Crying Game* on VHS and watched it with me when I was 10, and so I already knew before I knew the word "trans" that if I fooled a man into thinking I was a girl and tried to have sex with him he would think I was disgusting. I bet 1950s or 1850s girls like me didn't think of dysphoria as Cartesian, as a bad map drawn by a sick mind on a healthy body...but they might have.

And does it even make sense to call them trans girls if that category didn't exist yet. Another reason I'm stuck on this Foucault/Metzl idea about our categories being socially and culturally constructed is because I do feel trans-historical connection—like invisible ketamine vapor threads across time and space—to my sisters and to gender variant people, and I wonder what it means. Do I have to believe in some kind of non-verbal extracultural essence of transness? Would girls from other cultures and times relate to me too? Would girls in the 40s and 50s have thought that the most visible trans-femme celebrities of this year were symbols of liberation, or symbols of our identity being "discovered" and "invented" and colonized and controlled? Or both? or neither? And I guess, when I imagine hanging out with my sisters from other historical times,

I always wonder, would they have loved k?

One thing I feel writing this part is that I am mad and sad that people in academia write critical theory about the stuff I'm talking about here and then compete with each other in a capitalist marketplace for who has the smartest ideas at conferences and in journals. After I got depressed about this competition dynamic in my mid 20s I avoided writing about my ideas in public, because I didn't want to cheapen my own emotional experience or intellectual life by competing with it, commodifying it, saying that I had the best or right analysis, and then being validated by people on panels or at cocktail parties or in bars downtown. One of my teachers really helped me understand how this was wrong; she said, instead of writing think pieces, people should just write about how they are feeling, that would be more helpful.

Part of me writing this, of trying to make a map of the museum, is just because I was and am trying to not kill myself. Part of what helped me not do that so far was to write about some of these ideas. Cyrus, when reading this, asked why writing in particular helped and I don't know exactly but one possible reason is because it's like excavating my own mind (private symbols) and twirling something out of it that not everyone could see before (public symbols), and transition can also be like that—an excavation—so they compliment each other as processes. I did this twirling and decided to publish it mostly because my friend Clare asked me if I wanted to, and also because I thought maybe it could help some other girl not kill herself. Even if it's humiliating or self-commodifying for me to put this in the world, maybe it's worth it if just one girl reads this and doesn't kill herself. So that was the calculation I made. But I still think the academia/gender/theory/marketplace is mostly a garbage pile and a distraction from real social movement work. I also never want to contribute to a reality where someone feels inadequate or less-than because they haven't read Foucault or whatever. So if you felt that reading this, I want to say: the thing most people who read Foucault have in common, above all else, is expensive educations. Not wisdom, or insight, or superiority. Just to be really clear. And while I wrote this to talk to other trans people, and contribute to world where the stories of gender variant people are accessible to other gender variant people, I bet some day a cis person is going to want to argue with me about this section. And if you are that cis person, maybe instead of writing an argument, you should write about your feelings.

Anyways, when I have been sleeping with this person Aarti, and when we have sex, she doesn't like to touch my appendage. Hazel and I heard Mountain call their dick an appendage recently and it made both of us so happy so I have been saying it all the time. I love hanging out with Mountain and hearing what they think about and believe. Mountain said that gender is just a set of rules that you can adhere to more or less closely, with different advantages and disadvantages to your adherence, depending on a given situation. In this way, they said, it's like fan fic. But seriously, is it transphobia if a cis lesbian doesn't want to touch my appendage? Lately I have been seeing if something is transphobic by seeing if it makes me cry. I didn't want to cry about Aarti but maybe it's because we're not that close. I can't remember the *Everyday Feminism* article now, I don't care about that shit.

[meme I made in the fall of 2017 about the suicide museum. Every medical professional I've interacted with since I've come out, including some surgeon's assistants, have asked me if I have community or friends or people supporting me. These questions leave me with a fear that trans girls are isolated, and also a feeling of being lucky to have my special friends who keep me feeling like I'm real and valid, even if I'm crazy; i also sometimes feel like i'm ruining their lives, so then we have to process that too]

pt. iv, Miami (written sometime near Christmas 2017)

i have not talked to my mother about this manuscript and i am scared for her to ever read it or know it exists, and i wrote it thinking she would never read it

When I first came out to my mother (i really came out gradually to her over the course of months) she said "I don't want another daughter." I'm sitting in these silk panties from the 40s and a sports bra crying on a couch in Liz's apartment in downtown Miami. My mom just told me on the phone that she has cancer, or worse cancer than the doctors previously thought. I'm crying because my mom might die and we always thought my dad would die first, and I'm crying because my dad deadnamed me while we were on the phone talking about my mom's cancer and then corrected himself, and I'm crying because I feel so low capacity around being deadnamed by them, I feel so hurt by them, even though they're trying to really hard to be good trans affirming parents, it's funny how you can try so hard and still just not be the thing you want to be. I know so many parents are so much more horrible to their trans kids, I think about this as I cry.

I stayed up all night last night with Rebecca the therapist sitting in the hot tub at the fancy hotel where she is staying, also in Miami, and talking about her girlfriend, who also hung out with us at first and then went to sleep around 3am. Around 5am, probably, RTT (Rebecca the therapist) redirected the conversation from her troubled relationship with her girlfriend to my troubled relationship with my parents about trans stuff. I really went in telling her about my experience and it felt so intense, because we're really intense with each other, full eye contact and open bodies and both talking so fast and being so verbal, for so many hours.

The reason I'm crying right now on this couch, perhaps the weirdest and most illustrative thing about my thing with my mom, is that—even though she's given me a hard time about being a trap my whole life—the first thing I told her when we got on the phone was about staying up all night with RTT and how it made me feel, and even though my mom didn't really acknowledge what I had said or ask any follow-up questions, it felt special to get to tell her that, and it made me feel the feeling that I don't want her to die of cancer, even though I know I'm going to have years of struggle trying to be close to her as she comments on my body and my clothes and the surgeons I choose for my gender surgeries and the meds I take and the makeup I wear and my career choices and my girlfriends and boyfriends and friends who I'm just fucking and every other fucking thing in my life as though it's an act of love to comment on your kid's shit in a way that belies your anxiety about their transness, as though her worry for me is love. But even so, I can tell her about staying up late with RTT and that's somehow unspeakably meaningful.

Last night RTT—and many others before her—have told me that it's OK to be mad at my parents for being trans incompetent or trans illiterate, or transphobic, or trans clumsy, or whatever categorical trait you ascribe to someone when they make you feel horrible in your body and your gender when you're around them, even while they don't call you a faggot, or threaten to beat or rape or murder you (because my parents haven't done any of those latter things).

People tell me I am allowed to be upset, even if my parents aren't doing the worst, most violent things. I think my parents are sad that I'm a faggot trap bitch little girl and I think they think it's weird and gross and confusing and I don't totally know how to talk about it with them because they have a self-image of being progressive—because they are in a lot of ways—and they don't want to be wrong about their self-image, because it's very painful I think to have been wrong about something about yourself– and that pain on top of the pain of having been wrong about your kid in some deep way—and they were wrong about me, or I think my mom was really attached to my masculinity, and there was something off about that, now and also for my whole life—and so specifically their kid being a trap is just messing with them I guess.

Some trans people probably feel like they were wrong about something about themselves, maybe that's why they want to hide old pictures or documents that have their deadname or whatever. But maybe also they are just tired of getting shit for being trans, and you get less shit if your gender is cohesive and cis-reminiscent, without ancient photos that trace or describe a different gender presentation or different body. Trying to erase the dissonance that echoes like drone music from the trailer of an apocalypse movie through the halls of the museum. Sometimes when my mom is feeling stressed about my transness she reminds me that, in her language, I "was a boy before" and then

I wonder if it wouldn't be easier if I couldn't erase the dissonance for her, men-in-black-mind-eraser style, just cut the old memories out.

In the slasher comedy movie *Happy Death Day 2U,* the protagonist wakes up each day, gets murdered and has to start the previous day again. She finally stops the murder-repeating-day cycle only to discover she is in a slightly alternate reality where her dead mother comes back to life, but the boy she likes is dating her frenemy. She has to choose if she wants to stay in the bizarro world where her mother is alive but her lover is lost, or if she wants to live her gendered truth (through heterosexual monogamy) and have no mom. She chooses her gendered truth, because white culture really believes in killing (which practically often means jettisoning) one's parents. And so when I think about it being liberating to cut off my parents I also remember that this is part of what white capitalist individualism is telling me that my adult development can be, namely choosing my gendered truth over staying in the shit with my family of origin.

My mom was telling me about her cancer and I was asking her how she felt about it, and she said she felt scared and bad, in more words than that, and she talked about wanting to have a life where she got to do what she wanted, and a life that was long, and getting to meet my sister's kids, and my kids if I ever have any, and all this other stuff. And I kept thinking while she was talking: Will I ever be afraid to die?

Neither of my parents have ever told me about wanting to die explicitly, I guess except one time when I asked my mom what she believed about SSRIs and she said she took them to get rid of the dark thoughts that she sometimes has, and kind of alluded to suicide stuff, and I knew we were cut from the same cloth in some way, that she was telling me that she too had an altar to suicide that she had visited, or a river of suicidality in which she waded. Even when I don't go to the altar daily, I do pay my respects, periodically, with little offerings. Ideation, in the medical language, less or more planful, with or without means. I go in the museum and walk around. My father has told me many times that he is afraid to die or doesn't want to die, different versions of feeling aversion towards death, which makes so much sense and seems so normal, except he's also literally a philosophy professor who's written multiple books about people like Heidegger and Marx, and you would think that maybe someone who had done that kind of work in their life wouldn't be afraid to die? But whatever, he is, and no judgment. But also that's why I don't think theory can save me, because it didn't save my dad. He retired from being a philosophy professor and became a community mediator, because he thought that was *actually* helpful and redemptive. Maybe that's when it crossed over for him, maybe he started to love life and not want to leave it when he had kids and stopped doing existentialism. I should ask him.

It hasn't crossed over for me, or I feel and have felt like I wanted to die in different degrees, like sometimes a nagging itch or curiosity, like, just remembering that I could die on a given day, or other times a hunger, like a longing, wishing for death, visualizing it. Sometimes it's because I'm sad but sometimes I'm doing good and I still daydream about it. Walking in front of a train. Buying a gun and driving to Miami, or driving to miami and buying a Gun. Being in South Florida, drinking a can of seltzer, knowing the ocean is near, feeling so calm. Is there anywhere more beautiful to end it than Miami? In addition to the wish, there is a readiness, that I feel in near death situations, like when I'm on an airplane and it shudders hard in the atmospheric winds, I feel "I'm ready," even if I just had a good trip, even if I'm excited about what's next in my life. And everything sharper in this phase, like someone turned up the volume knob. And so in other parts of this writing when I talk about trying to prevent girls from dying or trying to prevent myself from dying, there is this other side of me that also believes it's a respectable choice to make yourself die, and I live with that belief too, that anyone who chooses death was doing their best, and did their best to make the choice to die with integrity, and that such choices, however tragic, should also be respected. When people say suicide is wrong, they are attempting to speak for the dead, and maybe this is a mistake.

Hazel sent me this text once (which appears in the meme below) about whether some day we would live in the trans commune with our different friends doing kids stuff and food stuff and our parents being interconnected too. And when I think about my parents being afraid to die and wanting to meet their grandchildren, I wonder if I will have a thing like that, like if I will have lifephase I get to eventually that makes me afraid to die, a life where I'm so rooted and interconnected and attached to the world that the idea of the world existing without me, or me not existing, or both of those things simultaneously, would feel fearful. It's not that I don't love life or feel addicted to certain parts of life sometimes, like feeling addicted to my friends or lovers or ketamine or the combinations therein, but I would feel OK leaving life. I guess that's the question I'm asking—will I always feel OK about leaving.

It's easier to talk about wanting to kill myself than it is to talk about my mom; it's hard to write about her, because it's hard to hang out with her, and even writing this I feel my pain about her pain about my transition, and how we're just ping-ponging pain back and forth at each other and not totally able to see each other whole. And maybe that's not exactly each of our jobs right now, or maybe it's never parents' and their kids' jobs to see each other totally whole, or maybe that's just something they aspire to but never quite touch. I wonder what I would see if I could see her whole personhood, not just see her as my mom. Part of the museum is not being able to see very far and so it makes it harder for me to comprehend her experience or do the heavy lift of teaching her about mine. And if I could teach her, what would I say, like, I'm addicted to k maybe we can get high together, and you can see how I don't exist, or you can feel more comfortable with my suicidality. Maybe I'm afraid that if she could really witness me she would be scared and sad. Or I guess one thing about my mom, no matter how much she hurts my feelings, is I know she doesn't want me to die.

There's this other echoing question for me as I ask this which haunts me like grey weather or chronic pain, the question, will I ever leave the museum, will I ever not be a glass mannequin transbitch always getting shattered, like I was telling RTT last night, with no attention for anything except close interconnection, druggy parties, and deep reflections about transness, will I ever go back to being a normal adult who goes to a job and does spreadsheets and does laundry and takes their dog to get heart medication at a veterinarian with magazines in the office, or literally whatever the fuck middle class cis people do because every day I have less and less of an idea. I was at the grocery store with Jamie in Oakland, shopping with her after yoga after her 9-5 job (I spent the day wandering around Oakland pretending to be shopping but really just wandering in and out of businesses hoping to be invisible and reading a book about trans people) and I said to her "I would be willing to have a 9-5 job like you, just if I never had to go to yoga alone and then the grocery store alone." "I know," Jamie says, "I always feel like an alien at the grocery store." I feel like an alien most of the time, when I see someone reading a magazine, or buying something in a store, I just have this feeling "What Are You Doing," alienated by everyone cis. I'm still lying on the couch in my underwear in Miami, thinking about what panties to wear to this queer party I want to go to, and if Hazel doesn't want to go with me what I will do, and how I am going to do k because I need that right now, and if Rebecca the therapist and her girlfriend will come. Maybe if I leave the suicide museum I would feel like my parents, afraid to die.

I keep thinking as I'm writing about this Nietzsche aphorism I read in college that seemed cool to me when I was 18, which is something like, "One should part from life as Odysseus parted from Nausicaa—blessing it rather than in love with it,"** or maybe like, "appreciative but not attached," or something like that. I think about that because it feels extremely bro-y, especially the invocation of an old seafaring warrior and a young princess, it's just like, come on. I'm obviously Nausicaa, hot, well-to-do, and obsessed with something that I can't grasp. But then there is the part of me, the part of me that told M (who I dated for like a year and some into my transition) when I was breaking up with them in the fall of 2017, that being trans made me feel a thousand years old, and how I do sometimes feel like an ancient seafaring bitch, wandering around making bad guesses about how to have a normal life and feeling sad. One time I was in a break up with a different ex, like years and years ago, and we were having sex in our friend's empty apartment in San Francisco in the middle of the night, having randomly met up even though we weren't supposed to be talking, and I had just been traveling for months. I had left the place we both lived because it was too much. I suddenly got visibly upset and she was like "what is it," and I just looked over in the corner at this big red backpacking backpack that I was living out of then, and said "my backpack," which was a symbol for me of wandering the earth alone forever, which is probably in some way what I will do, or I feel that way now, because my appetite for intimacy is like a forest fire and if I sleep in one place for too many nights I feel claustrophobic and weepy and I just leave. I don't want to be alone but I also just don't want to be a t all. My backpack. It might seem like your body is the problem, because your body goes with you everywhere too, but it's actually the museum.

Last night RTT asked me if I ever worried about what kind of relationship I was going to end up in, or if there was anyone out there for me, or what the deal was with that and I was trying to decide what to tell her, because I have a crush on her and want her to like me, slash I didn't want her to think I was psycho, and so I didn't want to say like "I know there are lots of people out there for me, but I don't know if there's ever someone who I won't ultimately abandon because I want to have a different life, and I've only ever really abandoned people or hurt them," because if I said that, then RTT might not ever want to kiss me or stay up late talking to me (My breakup with M felt like almost a caricature of this bad self-image I have, a crazy trap who hurts people by appearing so intensely and then disappearing). And it's intense with my crush on RTT, because in the suicide museum, romantic intimacy has been feeling bizarre and clownish, and I don't know how to deal with it totally. I'm totally addicted to crushes and getting obsessed with people, but aware of the inevitable horror movie ending, me being the angel of death who, through abandonment, rends the hearts of innocent lovers. And this partly because romantic obsession is not about the object in this phase, it's about the projection, I get hot for cis people whose gender it would feel safe to have, I get hot for trans people who seem less fucked up, I cling to the promise of something that would disconfirm my bad feelings. In any case, I think I did tell RTT some declawed version of the thing, and she was like "yeah basically same," but I wasn't sure exactly what she meant and if it was the same as me, because I had been vague and she had been vague and it was five in the morning and my plane had just landed in Miami like seven hours before and we had been sitting in a hot tub for the last three hours so I was pretty dehydrated and our conversation was a bit confusing.

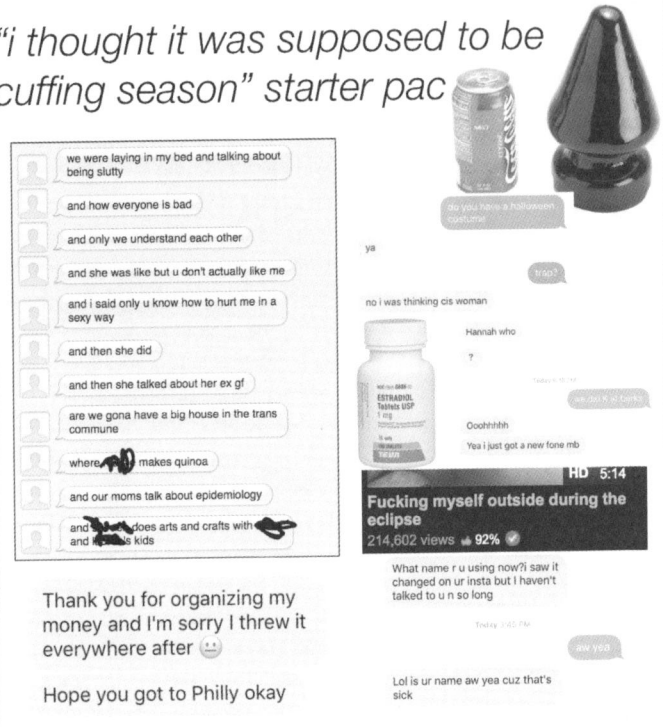

[meme I made in the fall of 2017, and it's about the suicide museum. Actually Hazel and a person she was dating at the time had a conflict about this meme, because the largest text on the left side is from Hazel, and refers to another lover of hers, and the current date saw this meme and figured out that Hazel had been seeing the other lover and was hurt. And that is the spirit of this time, too many lovers, too much pain.]

pt. v, just hanging out in the museum: january 14 2018

today i am a parody of myself, very high on ketamine on the chinatown bus in a bizarre outfit typing out this ridiculous thread on my laptop, which is on top of my legs which right now are wearing these insane dries van noten pants that really are like an acid trip, a floral brocade texture with an auburn and purple smear dripping over it, with little tinges of taupe. the pants look like a quilted magic eye. on my top I am wearing a giant iridescent purple down jacket, the precise color of which is hard to describe, like it just turns slightly green-gold in the sun, and again, it's huge and very puffy. under that I am wearing a grey wool and silk kimono/cardigan/robe article that I found in the basement of some downtown boutique, the belt of which hangs down far below the purple down jacket. underneath that I am wearing a navy blue uniqlo synthetic down vest, and under that this navy blue and white striped alexander wang sweater, which is also giant and boxy, and which hazel told me not to buy at the Saks in Miami when we were there for 10 days over christmas with Alivia acting like teenagers and doing acid in the ocean and ketamine in the rental car (and sitting in hotel hot tubs at dawn with certain jewish therapists). underneath the sweater i am wearing a pink pleated velvet mock-neck (i know it's hard to picture, just please picture it, each little pleat about a quarter centimeter apart and glistening like glass in the pink velvet, and it goes all the way up to my adam's apple) and then under that a grey velvet bodysuit, and under that a black lace thong, because Elizabeth taught me to wear underwear under my body suit so i don't have to wash the body suit as much. i forgot to mention i am also wearing a white rabbit fur snood and over that a navy blue paisley silk scarf which, when unwrapped, is probably five feet by five feet, and which Sam gave me when we were unceremoniously cheating on our respective monogamous partners senior year of college. I'm also wearing gigantic purple sunglasses I got from Steven Alan and black chelsea boots (Red Wings), and there is a purple and pink hair wrap braid in my blonde hair which is down and cascading over the navy paisley silk scarf and the white rabbit fur.

So I look like a crazy person. Which is funny because I got extremely high on k and then tried to get to the chinatown bus, not as a deliberate strategy, but just impulsively, I was getting so stressed trying to leave the house and I couldn't find my Juul, so I realized I had to go buy another one, but ALSO, I didn't say yet, my phone is broken, literally my lifeline to the world, my number one compulsive behavior device, my iPhone, has become a parody of itself, screen cracked beyond recognition, projecting all images in a hazy pink smear, and whenever I unlock it, randomly clicking and pressing itself, opening different apps, et cetera. I opened my messages and my phone, of its own broken volition, sensing ghost touches in its myriad cracks, attempted to facetime an acquaintance in west philly and my mother, before I turned it off—so I was trying to leave the house and trying to see if there was a place I could get my phone fixed or get my Juul fixed, and also thinking about maybe going to uniqlo and buying some warm layers and maybe some panties because all my girl underwear is dirty and even though I like the sleek boxer briefs I've always worn, they feel bad to me right now, dysphoric is maybe strong, but not what I want to wear, so I was like, maybe I'll get some of the panties I like at uniqlo or something, but then I LOST MY JUUL and my phone was broken, and I was just stumbling around my house in my panties and a navy blue sweatshirt that says "Balboa Island" trying to find my Juul and figure out what clothes I needed to pack to bring to New York, and also what other stuff besides clothes (for example my small tube of Kiehl's facewash, my perfume oil (bois de balincourt) and a diptyque shopping bag containing a strap-on harness, two different dildos, two bright red leather cuffs, two neon pink neoprene cuffs, a black leather collar, and some leather and brass clips to connect all of it) and I was throwing these things in a bag and thinking "where the fuck is my Juul"

if you don't know what a Juul is, it's a nicotine salt vaporizer the size of a USB drive that I started using after I met this cute stranger in LA and she was using a Juul after meals and stuff, and also after my mother told me that if I was going to get FFS I should really quit smoking cigarettes, which I have done, but am now just desperately addicted to my Juul, so much so that I had to buy another one today just because I couldn't find mine in my house

Coming down from the k now on the bus, thinking about doing k with Carolyn in my room a few days ago, how she asked if there's a k comedown and I said no, but thinking now that the incredible thing about k, or one of the incredible things, is like, because it's a dissociative, the experience of the comedown is actually an experience of integration and coherence, the blush of reality returning after the austere remove of k shimmers away. The bus is going through Camden, through really poor places, now through Cherry Hill,

New Jersey, and now just on 295 (a secret trick to save money driving from Philly to New York is to stay on 295 as long as possible before you get on the Jersey Turnpike, and then you pay less toll, Hazel taught me that, and her Jewish father taught her) the landscape going by and me slowly getting less high and trying to understand what's happening to me.

I still look like a crazy person in this outfit, and I really felt that earlier today when I was extremely blunted (that's the word Hazel says for being so high on k) and just wandering around Philadelphia after I finished wandering around my house. I wasn't actually wandering, I just had the errand of buying a Juul and then getting to the bus, and it could've been regular maybe. But I think the coil of anxiety that had built up as I tried to leave the house and pack and find my Juul meant that A. when I was getting dressed, instead of really packing clothes I just put on every single article of clothing I thought to bring, and B. when I was leaving my apartment, in the foyer, by a mirror adjacent to a radiator and another tenant's door, I took out my k and did a huge key bump. I walked about two blocks from my house, and realized I didn't have my wallet. I realized that I had emptied all the coins from my wallet out into the giant brass and ceramic vase on my dresser before leaving, and probably just left my wallet there.

So after taking all the things out of my enormous tote bag and out of my enormous pockets on the sidewalk, and realizing I had no wallet, I put all the things back into my pockets and bag and walked back to my house to get my wallet. This was all well and good but I still felt anxious and like an incompetent tranny freak of the earth who literally can't leave her house, so I did another bump of K when I was up in my room retrieving the wallet, and then I was really blunted. I could tell when I was walking down the street that people were looking at me funny, and I knew it was because I was trans white bitch wearing ridiculous shapes and colors and giant purple sunglasses and carrying a gigantic tote with dildos and laptop cables and clothes literally spilling out of it, and I didn't really *feel* anything at all about it, because that is the joy of k, it just made my feelings cool right down, and I walked to the El station and took the train to Center City.

On the train I realized I was really really high, like maybe so high it was weird I was in public. People would notice me and I was like "yes this outfit" but I definitely thought about how weird I looked less than I would have if I was not on k. On the train I was looking at a black person and thinking about my internalized white supremacy and how one of the markers of whiteness is that seeing a person of color *reminds you* of race, that you aren't just thinking of race already. I thought about my Russian and German and Latvian ancestors and how they didn't know about anti-blackness probably before they came to America, or at least in the way I know about it now, living in West Philadelphia– but these thoughts I'm describing, they weren't so verbal, they were just these extremely lucid and emotionally inert scans, like crisp transparencies on an overhead projector. Then I was noticing how I liked to think of myself as an individual, and as distinct and creative and clever and special—after all, if I wasn't a special individual, why would I write down all this shit about being a crazy trap in crazy clothes literally gripping onto the edges of life to keep it from sliding away from me—but when it comes to the fabric of white supremacy and capitalism, I'm no different, just part of a giant white supremacist tapestry that folds over on itself and twists into the architecture of material and ideological reality. If feeling like an individuated perceiving judging subject who masters reality is part of white supremacy, it's possible that what ketamine does is some component of unraveling the tapestry.

In this moment—just as I had this thought about my own lack of specialness and distinction from other white people, even though I'm an articulate, fashionable, over-educated tranny—I realized that there was a pane of clear plastic between me and the rest of the people in the train car, and that I could actually see my reflection ever so faintly, superimposed over the other people riding the El. While thinking I wasn't special, just a white bitch, and feeling that feeling, my face came into focus suddenly, my blonde hair and big sunglasses (because of course I was having this episode on the train underground with my sunglasses on). I think I used to work harder on "decolonizing" around my own white supremacy, which in a way meant being really reactive when I noticed myself doing quietly racist things (like letting a person of color "remind me" of race) and now in the trans girl suicide museum I am less reactive. I can describe my own racism and hope that I have more attention to work on it when I'm done not killing myself in 2020. I know that transitioning and being anti-racist or being an activist are not mutually exclusive, and probably a lot of the experiences I have as a trans person right now will help me with movement work and anti-racist work eventually. But when I was closeted I used to lead workshops for rooms full of do-gooders about antiracism, and now I can't even check out at the grocery store without being afraid of the cashier looking at my face, so it's hard to imagine standing in front of a room full of any people at all, let alone supporting them in their decolonization processes. I wonder when I will get the integration of coming down from this discarded exoskeleton of a life moment, when all this chaos will become some insight or useful expertise, when I will stop being insane and start being really tough and wise. The optimistic thing to believe would be something like 'hard times make people stronger,' but right now I just feel like I am balling up my painful experiences and throwing them into the corner of a room which is already filled with trash. Suicide museum.

Every time the train to Center City stopped I would think "Am I so high that I won't be able to know where I'm going" and kept repeating the address of the tobacco store in center city where I believed I could buy a Juul (my phone was broken remember? so i had to memorize the address), the address is 211 south 13th street (i think it's still there if you want to check it out). I'll get there eventually. But I would think to myself, am I too high, and then I would realize, no, I'm OK, I still know where the train is, and in Philly, the eastbound El counts down, so I got on at 46th street, and it would be 36th, and then 30th, and then 18th, and that was easy to know where I was in relation to 211 south 13th street.

Then suddenly the train got to 13th street, or to center city, I guess to 15th street, and I got off, and when I stood up felt the feeling of "jesus am I too high to be in public" and swung my gigantic tote around and hugged it in front of me so I could walk through the crowd of people on the subway platform with a buffer and also see if anything fell out of it. As I walked through the crowd, my visual field was extremely limited from being blunted, so I could only see a few things at a time, like my feet going up the steps out of the subway– I knew I was going up but I wasn't necessarily integrating the data between when I had looked up the stairs and when I had looked down at my feet going up the steps, so it was just "feet feet feet" and then WOW big bright sky when I came out. There was one part where I could see through this grate into a janitor's closet or like an area under construction or something, I couldn't really tell what it was because I was so high and also walking kind of fast, but I had this weird moment of being like "what the fuck why would they let me see into that janitor's closet, that would never be in the New York subway where everything is sealed off." Philly is messy like that, everything is broken and confusing, and the city tries to polish itself to appeal to developers and corporations, but at the end of the day it's just blunted trans girl burning through her savings trying to find her stuff in an apartment full of shit. New York is a cis straight couple, obviously.

I was walking in the bright open air and then feeling how shaded Center City Philadelphia is, like Kennedy Plaza in the winter when the low January sun doesn't ever get high enough to touch the sidewalk, you just see brightness on the tops of the buildings, and the geometry of the buildings was so concussive to my ketamine visual field, I just saw each and all of the blocks of each building, this gigantic self-reflexive totemic fractal in praise of artifice itself, with little architectural details like eaves and cornices on just some of the buildings, and inside all the wiring and ducts and pipes and shit, and as I looked at all the shapes, I fingered and turned my tiny glass bottle of perfume oil in my pocket, and felt it's geometry, and my finger sensations matched all the giant buildings' tiny geometries, and I scorned the buildings for making the sun dim and grey and not able to touch the ground, and felt the pitifulness of the city, the way in which the tall buildings in a grid are just a big toy that some white men put together on stolen land, a monument to men who love money, and not even a place where the air and light feel open, just a drab fortress of grey winter shade.

I was trying to walk to the vape store, and kept being surprised that I knew where I was, that I knew where I was going, because my brain was like crusted salt on the winter sidewalk. On the walk I kept seeing people panhandling, sitting on the sidewalk bundled up, in piles of their stuff, sometimes with signs asking for money, sometimes just sitting. Since transition, talking to any stranger in public had become fearful, and so I was surprised by a feeling of closeness to the people sitting on the sidewalk, a feeling that in my own drug-haze-walking-pile-of-stuff-spilling-everywhere-sick-brain-broken-brain state I was close to someone sitting on the sidewalk, that if I didn't have somewhere to go, I too I would be sitting, so high and having no real sense of anything besides my body moving through the streets, floating almost, dead to everyone, with all my important possessions in my arms, living in the consequences of choices I'd made trying to avoid depression and death. the feeling was so strong the second or third person sitting in the street I saw, I took out my wallet and gave them a five dollar bill, and then had this flash thought about being a rich white person who puts on weird clothes and does drugs and imagines what it's like to be homeless, and I think if I hadn't been high on k—addicted to k—I would have felt tremendous scorn and shame towards myself, but in my highness just referenced my own positionality in a flash—like 360° of my video game avatar with all my stats—and reminded myself to be humble and kept walking.

When I got to the Juul store I was still so high. I did not know what the store would be like or what was going to happen to me there. If you go to the Juul website they tell you all the retail locations where you can buy a Juul and this was the closest one to the chinatown bus. My last act of reason before my spiral was finding this store's address. Inside it was extremely strange. Floor to ceiling cigar cases and all cis men sitting around smoking cigars. There was a bar, but behind the bar only giant jars of tobacco, no booze. It seemed like there was a sports thing happening on TV. I looked around, and had this flashing feeling like maybe I would get murdered by these men, so when one of them, indistinguishable from the rest, asked me if he could help me, and I realized he was an employee of the business (what a dream, to work somewhere and be almost indistinguishable from the clientele; like selling ketamine to your friends at a party) I dropped my voice down so I would look like a faggot and sound like a man, instead of looking like a faggot and sounding like a faggot. I told him I wanted to buy a Juul and he got up from a deep leather couch and opened a giant glass cigar case and pointed me to the shelf with the Juul and its accessories. "Just take whatever you want" he said and I took what I needed and looked around the room, through the haze of cigar smoke and at all of the lit up cigar cases and the different men watching sports and thought "this is an incredibly special place," but also had this peculiar feeling, perhaps related to what I felt seeing the panhandlers, of knowing that I couldn't stay there, that the place was special but that I wouldn't want to rest there, that it was wrong for me, that I needed to keep going. Odysseus and Nausicaa at the same time. When I left, after paying for the Juul with my credit card (credit cards are crazy, I remember thinking, like a money wand, a clandestine portal of money, a small flat spell-casting agender money penis) I no longer felt like the men were going to murder me and I was also so shocked and relieved to have acquired another Juul.

Other times when I have desperately bought a Juul because of nicotine deprivation / lost Juul problems, I have shredded open the packaging on the sidewalk outside the store, desperate for a hit. But this day I knew the Juul would be very intense for me, and I was so high, not ready for nicotine yet. I put my bag down on the sidewalk outside the vape store and looked for my purple sunglasses for a few minutes, trying desperately to find them in my pockets, in my bag, et cetera. When they emerge from my purple iridescent down jacket pocket in a tangle of my keys, some headphones, and a vial of ketamine, I felt immense relief. I put the sunglasses on and realized they were helping me be in the world so much, they were saving me. No one can see my eyes.

On the bus writing this, I thought about this activist Ray, I met at a conference for young people working on wealth redistribution. She is an organizer who did not grow up rich and I felt really moved by some of the things she said about her work and about social movements and about rich people and poor people, utterances which, if I repeat them here, I might cheapen them or not convey their total weight, so I will just say that I felt connected to her and that she asked if I wanted to go visit her in the place where she lives and I did want to, and said I did.

I felt a strong pull to her, a specific kind of attraction that shakes me to my core, when someone I respect or admire as a thinker or an activist expresses that they value my personhood. It happens so rarely and always melts me like wax, and I felt totally melted by Ray and her invitation to come visit. We emailed a little bit after the conference, first in a work capacity, but then I asked how she was doing and how she felt in the winter (this was maybe six weeks ago, and the conference maybe ten weeks ago?) and she said I should email her on her personal email account and asked what I was doing with the winter, and told me what novels she was reading, and I just felt so fucked up about trans ness and class and how completely cut off from my political or activist life I've been in the suicide museum, just going to no protests and no planning meetings and systematically neglecting any relationship with anyone who would pull me back into activist work, because I have no constitution for it, no imagination for it, just imagination for myself, my clothes, my drugs, my friends, my fucked up gender, my surgeries and health insurance and did I mention clothes, my web browser is all 60 tabs of Issey Miyake and 12 tabs of Wendler's glottoplasty longitudinal research determining that MTF traps do experience a noticeable improvement in the pitch of their voice ("improvement") after getting the surgery, Yohji and how injectable estrogen may block testosterone better than oral, but also is often in short supply, Dries and can I get an appointment at the trans clinic this week and do I need to call them or can I just think about it a lot and then maybe go there one day when I feel good about leaving the house .-.-.- and what's more pathetic than a rich person who uses luxury clothing to locate herself ;;; my sense of myself as a political person, an agent who participates in movements, is totally shrouded by the dark irony of feeling so unsure if I even exist that I need my apparel to reflect my identity back to myself, the crutch of the esoteric and/or expensive clothes because any other way to relate to myself is too painful.

I'm so scared to write to Ray my activist friend and tell her that I'm a stupid rich trash bitch who only thinks about transexuality and couture. I don't think she would even be mad, she would be like "what's going on in your process" or something generous insightful, but I'm doing a lot of projection, and I feel scared to get close to people who care about movement work right now, because I feel so much shame about my own remove and I imagine them putting feeling that towards me too. Cyrus says if I don't want to do activism right now I can really own that and stop being hard on myself about it. I'm trying to do that but I feel bad for not facilitating meetings and setting up phone trees and flyering for events and trying to recruit people to help with stuff, and all the other shit I used to do. Part of the shame I feel towards Ray is the feeling of wanting her to absolve me, of wanting someone external to tell me it's OK that I'm a bimbo (and/or extremely low capacity) and some part of me knows that I can't ask anyone else to do that, no one else can soothe this one. I re-read Ray's email on the bus ride hunched over my laptop in my clownish outfit; I can't bring myself to write her back today.

By the time the bus got to New York I was not as high anymore and I went to Elizabeth's apartment and she held me while I cried.

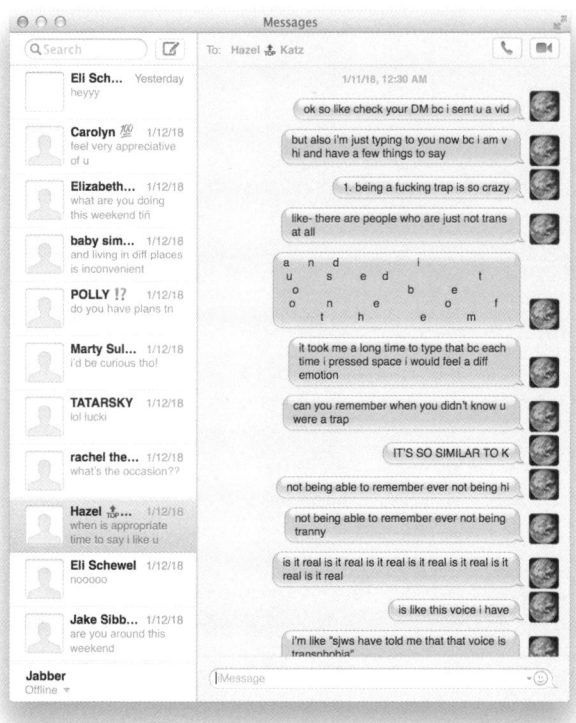

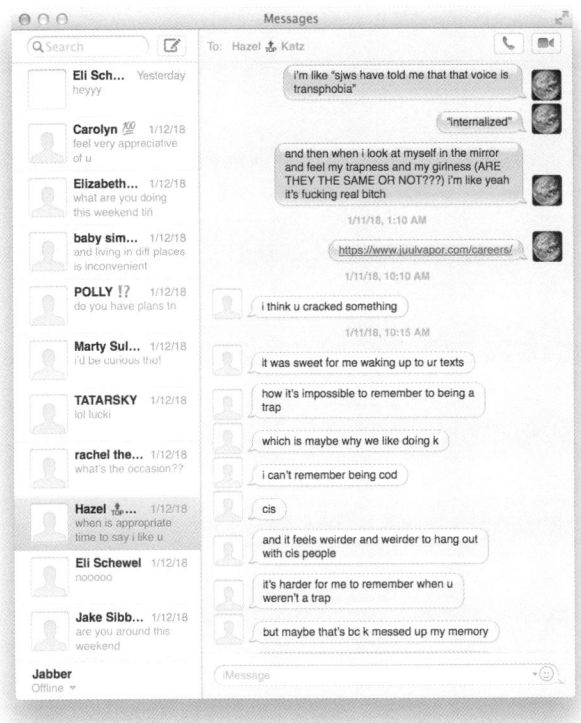

[texts i sent to hazel when i was trying to clean my room but did ketamine instead.]

pt. vi, how to get asked your pronouns (suicide museum underwear drawer guided tour)

[texts with Hazel about when my Juul broke the night before]

The first professional space where I was out as a trans girl was a group relations conference in New Orleans last summer. I was not using the name Hannah yet, but went to the conference everyday wearing a full face of makeup, and dressing like how I like to dress. There was no ritual at the conference about saying pronouns so people were confused about how to deal with me, like what gendered mode to use to relate to me. A few queer people in the space and some of the people of color tried to connect with me. A few months after the conference, Cyrus and Hazel and I were at a very fancy party (with movie stars and a red carpet) and we ended up in the corner with a bunch of black people and bunch of trans people, and Cyrus whispered: "Isn't it interesting how all the black people and all the trans people end up in the same corner," and I agreed that it was interesting but did not want to extrapolate past that, because I didn't want to do the thing that white queers with class privilege sometimes are tempted to do, where we align ourselves with disempowered people as a way of avoiding being in the undesirable role of oppressor.

At the group relations conference there was one moment where a queer woman who is also a social justice educator tried to get everyone in the group to say their pronouns during the middle of this open space-y all-conference dialogue. My body was filled with terror. I didn't know why. I just knew everyone else (maybe 60 people) in the room was cis, or at least cis passing. These were mostly consultants, HR professionals, MBA students. A gay man in the group told me later that he was disappointed I didn't say my pronouns during that moment, that he felt like I left everyone hanging. I didn't know how to explain to him that I couldn't breathe in that moment, that I felt terror of being out to the group, being the only trap and having to name it. That was even, like, before I was totally in the museum. I was still trying to exist in professional spaces, trying to relate to normies.

To this day, especially now that I use the name Hannah, I sometimes resent being asked my pronouns. It annoys me when crotchety old university professors, or sweaty cis republican men critique pronouns as part of introductions, because they don't understand how healing it can feel and how important. When I first started using 'they' pronouns I was so moved by being able to out myself as maybe—perhaps, potentially, tangentially, plausibly—someone who was considering myself not cis in a given space. All I had to do was shave my face smooth and say I used 'they' pronouns and then suddenly the other queer and trans people would be open to connecting with me. It felt like a miracle, the ease with which I could slowly inch towards transition in this way.

But now that I like she/her pronouns, and just want people to think I'm a hot girl, it's different. I experience my own foucauldian terror of having to be assimilated or interpreted anytime I enter a space, supposedly to protect *me* from getting misgendered (one of my first memes was about this, printed at the opening of the last chapter of this book). If being told my pronouns prevented people from misgendering me, maybe I would care more about introducing myself with them. But it doesn't help. Trans and queer people recognize me and do it right regardless and cis people misgender me, no matter how many times I say "she or they is fine," when asked my pronouns, which is what I say, the "fine" to convey that I resent the ritual.

I know trans people are supposed to get to be trans no matter how they look or present. This is why the pronouns ritual is supposed to be important, to let you introduce yourself without anyone's assumptions interfering with your wish. But I also know that hearing someone's pronouns doesn't make a cis person witness their gender. And this is part of the trauma. As Cyrus told me so long ago, gender is constituted in part by what's reflected back to you, and you don't get to instantiate the exact reflection you want just by saying your pronouns. That's why I'm having my face cut open.

When I was at the group relations conference I made friends with an older cis woman from Miami, Sophia, a rich lady who worked for an arts foundation. Sophia and I quickly found that we loved to talk to each other, and stayed up late telling each other about our families, our lovers, our sisters' dead ex-husbands, about career and psychology and art and her BMW. I had not yet come out to my parents, so was not yet fighting with my mother about my transness. But I was looking for trans-affirming mother figures, aware that there was going to be a storm when my mom finally had to face me. Spending time with Sophia was extremely gender affirming, she liked me as a young woman, liked my jokes and relational style, liked my tenderness and seriousness, liked my outfits. The last night of the conference we were getting drunk in a rooftop bar in New Orleans and we were talking about her sex life in her first marriage. We ordered another round of drinks and I told her, I think, that I didn't know if I would ever get married, because who wants to marry a trans person, and also because I was suspicious of marriage. (She was unmarried at that point too, had been unable to conceive because of her mother taking that horrible drug from the 50s that made their children barren–See?! we were talking about real girl stuff). At this point the conversation turned to my transness, and she was drunk for the first time. It's interesting, she noted, because you dress like a boy sometimes, referring to a day in the conference when I wasn't wearing a dress, but instead tight white Dana Lee jeans and a navy blue linen Linder baseball-style button up, and I think white Danskos. I suddenly felt shocked. White jeans and a blue blouse was not boy clothes. I was just dressing like a hot dyke. I was just dressing down. We were sitting in the rooftop bar both wearing drapey black floor length clothes, because we were both hot fun art bitches, drinking mezcal cocktails and talking shit. I suddenly felt in this moment the reality that my clothes were my gender calling card, more than my pronouns, more than whether or not I paid a surgeon to cut my dick off. A single crack in the veneer, a single day not wearing a dress, and I was suddenly a boy again. I went to the bathroom and touched up my lipstick.

These psychologists studied how people identified gender by showing research subjects hundreds of drawings of people with varied gender identifiers, people with both boobs and dicks, mustaches and pussies, fat hips and crewcuts.** They asked subjects to identify the gender of the person in each image, and to say how sure they were of the gender they perceived. They found that the penis was the strongest identifier, in that the penis, more than any other marker, contributed to people's *certainty* that they had correctly identified the gender. If someone had a pussy and full beard, respondents might say woman or man, but they would say they weren't sure. If the drawing had a dick, people were sure. Masculinity is the default, and dicks are the tell. The psychologists did not have the people's preferred gender pronouns on the drawings. The drawings were naked people, no clothes to use as identifiers.

I don't know what to do about my dick in my clothes, though Uniqlo makes these compression panties shaped like boxer briefs for women who feel fat, and they make my dick press up against my body. I like this, but I also like thongs, which are trickier. Some of the thongs I wear are high-waisted because the extra fabric makes it so that I have to have somewhere to put my penis. Unless they have a tight elastic waistband, low-cut thongs fall down and my dick falls out. I learned this the hard way, borrowing Elizabeth's underwear. It's a weird feeling walking around with lace around your hips and in your ass, but your penis dangling out, swinging around in your pants or dress. High-waisted thongs, as long as you don't put them in the dryer, don't have this problem, they have enough fabric to hold my penis and testicles, and enough friction with my body not to slide down. When I was having a crush on Lily last spring, I was afraid my dick would get small and not be hot to her. Now I want my dick to shrivel up so I can wear cute underwear.

When I was a kid, my mom always gave me hand-me-downs from her friends' kids, and one time tried to give me hand-me-down underwear, white Hanes briefs that had belonged to an older boy from another family. I told her I didn't want the hand-me-down underwear and she assented, saying that I didn't have to wear them. I'm actually surprised that she assented, in retrospect, because she didn't like when I did fussy, expensive-taste behaviors as a child. I guess she did kind of out me as not wanting the under in front of the mother from the other family, whose son originally had the underwear, and I remember feeling embarrassed for not wanting it, and confused about underwear.

When I was eighteen and living in a rural place, I ordered a pair of underwear from International Male, these UNICO brand trunks with horizontal white and navy stripes, like a sailor. I loved these panties so much and wore them threadbare, and began only wearing UNICO boxer briefs from then on. Only since this part of my transition have I tried to find other underclothes, long after I started wearing dresses and makeup. I started wearing bras too, before I started wearing femme panties. The last time I went to Aarti's house I wore a thong for the first time with her, lace and high-waisted and crimson, and when we were kissing in our underwear she grabbed my ass for the first time, slid her hands into my black oversized Vibskov trousers and gripped my butt, and I felt sexy in my new panties.

In my early teens, maybe eleven or twelve, I secretly bought a tiny white thong from a department store and wore it alone in my room, wishing I *could* wear it but always feeling like it was wrong. I remember thinking I could wear it out of the house, but I would definitely get caught, and the cost of getting caught would outweigh any potential enjoyment of wearing the underwear I wanted to wear. Remembering this tiny thong helped me do Cyrus's mom's instructions, remembering what I would have worn every day of my life as a girl (see the following chapter about mothers). If I had been allowed to be a teenage girl when I was actually a teen, I would have worn thousands of thongs, thongs sliding up over lowcut jeans, thongs in my soffe shorts, thongs in my pajama shorts with matching camisole; no one would have asked my fucking pronouns.

Introducing pronouns, as a practice is perhaps an appeal for everyone to be seen publicly in relation to their preferred private symbol. I want to tell people my I use 'lace thong pronouns,' I use 'ketamine princess' pronouns, I need people to know that my pronouns are 'she/her/suicidality.' I want my pronouns to be "sorry/i got/lip gloss/on your dick" or "yes/you can fuck me/but i'm just going to lie here" or maybe I'll tell people my pronouns are "yes you can come over / and yes I'll give you K / but please don't fucking try to touch my disgusting perfect transexual body." I don't want anyone to think they are entitled to an explanation of how I related to my gender and my body, and sometimes when I'm asked my pronouns I feel like that's what people are asking for.

Do trans girls understand sexism? Perhaps Sophia was doing sexism to me when she thought I was boyish for wearing jeans one day of our week together. Do cis girls immediately stop being girls if they dress like dykes for one day? Hazel bought her four-year-old nieces children's make up for Christmas and her cis sister-in-law (cister?) was appalled, not because of the makeup itself, but because how could Hazel, a trans girl, understand how makeup can be problematic. Hazel told me that no one—her sister-in-law or anyone else in her family—asked her what her relationship to makeup was, no one asked her if she wore makeup to pass or if she liked makeup. She told me she bought the makeup for her nieces because they love femme stuff. Her brother said when they opened the present they looked up and exclaimed "finally!" (they're four, and twins). Hazel said the twins would have to negotiate it eventually, and that it seemed like a sweet thing to get for them, that they would get to grow up and decide their relationship to it. Her sister-in-law didn't want a transgirl being the ambassador of femmeness, didn't want someone supposedly unhurt by sexism to be the guide. When guys on grindr send me pictures of their dicks along with messages about how I'm passable or beautiful or look like a real girl, I know that trans girls experience sexism too, even if it's different. When I was a cis guy on grindr, I just got the dick pics.

I know transmisogyny is real, obviously, but part of the brainwash that I experience/d from identity politics spaces and also just internalized transphobia is never being sure if it's real, if I'm secretly just an entitled man on hormones who loves his tiny boobies and his lingerie and who shouldn't get to talk about sexism because it's a system he benefits from. I'm trying to practice talking about sexism.

pt. vii, trans girl suicide museum 3: hall of mothers

Cyrus's mom is a photographer and one time we were in the Providence Place mall together (me and Cyrus's mom, both visiting Cyrus at school) I think in 2013, in J. Crew, looking at women's clothes. And I said to Cyrus's mom, I have been wondering lately how I would dress if I was a girl (because I was not out yet, but that was the kind of "cis guy" I was, wandering around the women's section at a J. Crew talking about being a girl with my friend's mom, aka a closeted trans girl). Cyrus's mom said to me something about a photography thing she had worked on, where she photographed these adult-human-size dolls.

"It was hard to figure out what the dolls were going to wear" she told me. She described her process trying to dress them and thinking through their wardrobe choices. Her breakthrough moment in dressing the dolls was realizing that in order to know what they would wear on a given day, she would have to know what they wore the day before, and the day before that, and the day before that, all the way back to the first clothes they ever wore. "If you wanted to know what you would wear as a girl," she told me, "you would have to go back and figure out what you would have worn as a girl each day of your life." She paused and looked at my outfit—grey Patrick Ervell sweatpants, a grey sweatshirt with a picture of Rihanna on it, and a shiny black plastic coat that looked like a garbage bag, and black Nikes—and added "also, like what you would wear in real life as a girl, not just in your imagination of being a girl – like what you would wear if you were at the mall with your friend's mom, which might not be that different from what you're wearing right now." In that moment I didn't understand that I was experiencing something I would later call "trans-affirming." 'You may already be doing your preferred gender expression' Cyrus's mom was telling me.

Thinking about going back to all the girl outfits every day of my life, like scrolling through tabs on an iPhone web browser, each one slightly different than the last. In this phase of my transition I am reliving a femme adolescence, only wearing thongs and mesh shirts with my bra showing, waxing my body hair and getting manicures. I think of the phrase "baby trans" and how Cyrus's mom's advice gives this phrase a new light, that a recently out trans person is a baby because they have to go near their gender at every part of their life in order to be "adult trans." I know there's more to gender than clothes, but clothes is a big part of it for me right now, maybe because it makes me feel peaceful, I can fully dissociate when I'm just looking at and touching clothes, and when I'm wearing the right clothes I feel good in my body and my gender and don't worry as much about getting screamed at in a bathroom. Also the thing I said before about fancy clothes being this demented way to locate myself when I'm dislocated, bimbo road map to museum no one goes to but you.

I have been making a joke in my head lately that I am reclaiming "bimbo," that I am an unabashed advocate for ditziness. It's hard to explain, I am just trying to survive right now, but sometimes I worry I am just a rich girl thinking about how to dress myself, how to dress a new doll, and how could these be the stakes of my survival. I go visit Cyrus's mom and we talk about clothes for hours. She doesn't like shopping at small boutiques because they don't have consistent return policies. She prefers Bergdorf's or Barney's. She asks me what I think about Antifa. I am sitting in her kitchen in rural Connecticut, where everything is matte white or glossy white and glass windows open onto a manicured estate, replete with a gardener, trimming massive hedges. It's the end of the summer, 2017. I tell her that Antifa are portrayed negatively in the media but that I believe they're a really important component of resistance. Also that it's not one bloc with one set of beliefs, but that different people believe different things, and that this diversity of perspectives and tactics is part of the strategy. I think I said "it's a tendency," which I do believe, but was also maybe not super meaningful to her. She tells me that the Antifa people she saw at the women's march were scary, that they were masked up and seemed like they wanted to get into trouble. I agreed that sometimes they were scary. I didn't tell her how I like a ski mask instead of a bandana because of how it tucks into my hoodie, or which fanny pack I use to store my black clothes when I need to change quickly after an action. I don't tell her about the charges the J20 protesters face, nor do I tell her that if some of my friends saw me sitting in her kitchen talking about shopping, they would feel betrayed. I wondered if she would feel betrayed thinking about me destroying property. I think about my mother feeling betrayed that I identify as a girl, my mother saying "I don't want another daughter."

Cyrus's mom wanted to talk to me about facial feminization surgery because she knows a lot of people who have had aesthetic surgery on their faces. I agreed because I love her, and she has been very supportive of my transition. She asks me about what procedures I want to get done, and I begin describing the typical components of FFS, starting with upper-third of the face. As soon as I mention rhinoplasty, she interrupts me. "You have such a beautiful nose, Hannah." I try to explain that if I reduce the protrusion of my forehead, my nose will be disproportionately large. "They're going to try to get you to do everything, they always do," she says, "they're going to give you a menu of options, and you don't want to do all of them, you don't need all that stuff." She suddenly seems distressed. "You have a beautiful face," she wants me to know, "you look so beautiful." She talks about women her age (60s-70s) getting surgery and how it's different for me, because I'm so beautiful.

Cyrus's mom was the first, but certainly not the only cis woman to give me advice about how to do gender affiring surgeries. And the advice she was giving came in a spirit of love, which I understood, and which made it easier to hear. At the same time, I didn't know how to tell her that I'm not getting the surgery because I want to look prettier, that I'm getting it so I can pass, so that I can be slightly safer, so that bathrooms and parking lots and bus stations and restaurants and subway platforms and street corners and even mansions in Connecticut could be just places rather than invitations to hyper-vigilance, sites of tension and sweaty palms and darting eyes. I explained this to Rebecca the Therapist in the hot tub in Miami, too— I think I will look hot and feel good after I get surgery on my face, but I also need to get it so I can just walk around without being so fucking afraid. Dysphoria is not merely about wanting to be hot, nor about my sick brain in my healthy body— it's about daily threats of violence, about not being witnessed or interpolated as I want to, and the ways people react when *they* feel fear about your transness.

Cyrus's mom and I are on the phone, she's on speaker phone and Cyrus and I are in a liquor store near Redlands, California. She's saying about how so many of her friends get too many procedures done. Cyrus can tell I feel uncomfortable being compared to a cis woman seeking ideal beauty standards, and he takes he takes the phone and gives his mom an appreciation, says we need to go because we're at our friend's house, but that we really appreciate her talking to us. Cyrus's mom says that I should send her my surgeon's name, and that I should hire a nurse for the first forty-eight hours after surgery to help me recover. Cyrus says thank you mom. I say thank you thank you thank you.

Cyrus's mom has not had an easy time with Cyrus's transition; she was attached to the idea of having a daughter and disturbed by the idea that her "daughter" would want to cut his breasts off, would want to use the name Cyrus. She has gone through different phases of support and anxiety, and Cyrus is so forgiving of her, in a way I have not been able to be with my parents. Over time she has become very supportive of him.

Right before the bad phone conversation, Cyrus's mom asks to photograph me. She wants to body paint me, to have artists paint jeans and a t-shirt onto my body, like a Sports Illustrated shoot. I agree. Cyrus asks, do I think she's objectifying trans people. I don't know, I say, maybe, but it's validating. Cyrus's mom tells me I have a beautiful body and how excited she is to photograph it. I so rarely feel beautiful, I'm touched that would say that. In January 2018 I stand up for five hours in Cyrus's bedroom in the family apartment in New York City, with two cis women strangers painting me. I am wearing nothing but a thong and then the painted-on jeans and painted-on white t-shirt. The artists are using she pronouns for me, but one of them accidentally calls me "he". She has just been painting blue jeans onto my thighs and crotch, dabbing a paintbrush on the bulge in my underwear. I don't feel angry that she misgendered me for some reason. I feel appreciative of her, generous even, towards Caitlin from New Jersey, living with her mom and her step-siblings and body painting people as her job, dabbing my penis through my underwear with a paintbrush, trying to get my grey jersey thong the color of denim.

We are in this fancy apartment and they are renovating in the next unit and there is this loud shaking grumbling sound on and off throughout the hours they are painting me. Caitlin complains about the noise. "I guess it's a rich people thing," I say, "constantly renovating your home." Caitlin and the other body painter can't stop laughing at this remark, this commentary that names richness as a phenomenon. The room we are in has probably 17-foot ceilings and a gigantic window that looks out on the skyline. I suddenly am on their side, a person noticing richness, rather than just living it. I try to codeswitch around class all the time in this way, richer than my poor friends and less rich than my rich friends. Richer than Caitlin, less rich than Cyrus's mom, less and more of a woman than either. Maybe I don't mind Caitlin misgendering me because I feel superior to her because of class stuff. Maybe it's just because she's been really nice to me all day. I can't totally tell.

When they finish painting my body they paint my face, or do my makeup, a "beauty" look, they keep saying, which I deduce means, simply, regular makeup. Caitlin mixes paint in the airbrush gun to spray on my forehead, my cheeks, my chin. She mixes the paint carefully to match my skin. Then Cyrus's mom takes me into another room and puts her own high heels on me, these suede black stilettos, too small for my enormous feet. Suddenly she realizes that my toenails are not painted. She laughs and runs into the other room, and then sits on the floor in front of me with a tiny jar of red and paints each of my toes. I am painted head-to-toe. I love this moment when Cyrus's mom is attending to me like this, touching my body like I am her daughter, when I am no longer being painted by an employee, but being painted by the matriarch. I think about how it felt for Cyrus as a child, having such a powerful mother, who gives such focused, loving attention.

Cyrus's mom shoots me sitting on a stool in front of bright lights. She gives me femme cues, "point your toes towards one another," "bring your knees closer together," "chin down," "don't smile, but think about a smile." The pictures make me feel a wave of warmth, I look like a hot girl. "You're beautiful" she tells me, "your transition is important to me." It feels so loving I don't know how to explain it. It reminds me of a thing I tell myself when I am in my grad school class, the only trans person, feeling like a fucking alien, which is that it can feel like a miracle to be close to a trans person, that seeing a trans person living in their gender the way they want to can be like seeing a magical apparition, a gasping oxyenated tear in the asbestos-insulated lining of normal gender. "It's actually a very beautiful thing to even get to see a trans person let alone talk to them," I want to tell my grad school classmates staring at my big hands and my tiny tits, "like it is a real gift and people should treasure it, because honestly nine times out of ten i'm in my room blowing k alone, so you're basically beating the odds if you get to chill with me, especially since I'm not dead yet." Maybe this is hate us, want to hurt us, because we're so beautiful.

The day after the shoot I see Cyrus's mom again and she offers to buy me the shoes of hers that I was wearing, these black Stuart Weitzman stiletto sandals. "They're like a basic, every girl needs them," she tells me. She asks me if I'm still going to get FFS. It's been almost 3 months since the phone conversation where I felt misunderstood by her. Yes I tell her, I'm still going to get it. She pauses and then asks if I want her photoshop guy to feminize my features in the photographs. "I was nervous" she said, "that you wouldn't want these pictures in public because I shot you before you had the surgery." I feel so moved by her offer, by her understanding of the anxiety I might have about it. "I love the pictures," I tell her, "you don't have to change them at all. They're a record, and you made me look hot." "You're beautiful," she tells me again.

My mom has not yet told me I look beautiful. I think she thinks trans girls are ugly, or as she would say, "weird." The morning of the Antifa conversation with Cyrus's mom I was wearing impossibly large and gratuitously textured silk black and navy garments, and texted a picture to my mom, because I was going to a wedding later that day: "this is my wedding outfit." "I don't see why you have to look so goth," my mom replied. I don't explain to her about the dolls, having to figure out what they would have worn each day, the day before and the day before that, all the way back to their childhoods. I haven't even gotten all the way back to my childhood, I want to tell her. When I was small I had a quilted red and white silk skirt with tiny navy paisley on it, that was my favorite thing. I was four. I wore it everywhere. One time I wore it to CVS with my father and my older sister and we ran into some kids from the family daycare my sister and I went to after preschool. My sister was embarrassed to have her younger sister be someone who everyone thought was a brother, or she narrated it as her younger brother wearing a skirt in public. This story became a legend in my family for no clear reason; 'the time Hannah wore a skirt to CVS and Addie was embarrassed' gets brought up every so often. Everyone thought it was a funny story. My family tells fewer of these stories in this phase.

I remember when I was a kid I was very aware that my mother didn't shave her legs or armpits. I remember walking into her bathroom once, seeing her with a magnifying mirror, tweezing her chin hairs. What are you doing, I asked. Tweezing my chin hairs, she said matter-of-factly, in a matter-of-fact tone she uses sometimes when she is defensive. Why do you tweeze your chin hairs if you don't shave your arms or legs? I asked. She seemed annoyed. Because I don't want to look like a man, she said.

I was extremely high on K with Goda lying on my bed in west Philadelphia, watching Hazel's documentary about retirement communities, when I went to the bathroom and looked at my gay-ass faggot face in the mirror. I'm so excited to get FFS is probably what I was thinking. Why don't I want to just look the way I look, I thought. And then, in a magical ketamine skip, I remembered my mother's annoyed words to me as a child, seemingly annoyed that I was questioning her gender presentation (and to be fair, someday, if I have a child that I read as a boy, and I have endured a life of sexism, maybe it will annoy me if he seems to be questioning my gender presentation). Remembering this moment, I began to laugh, because I realized my second-wave feminist mother and I have something in common: neither of us want to look like a man.

I'm writing about Cyrus's mom and listening to rap music on my headphones—thinking about how Hazel and I joke about transphobic cis women being mad at us for listening to sexist rap music, like how our moms would probably say that real girls wouldn't like sexist music—on a train to see my family in Santa Barbara, it's February 2018. I'm going to see Cyrus in LA after Santa Barbara and hoping that the visit with my family is not too hard. Claudia asked me what my self-care strategies were for seeing my parents and being trapped on vacation with them. I tell her I brought two 8-balls of k on the airplane. What else she asks. I have no other plan. The train is stopping in Merced and the conductor says we can get off and smoke a cigarette (I'm just smoking my Juul in my seat) but cautions us not to go into the station–

"we don't want to leave without you"

Some wing of the suicide museum, or of my suicide museum, is about parents. I know not everyone has parents. But if you do, when you die young, some part of you cuts off some part of your parents' legacy. I don't believe in "nature" beyond how we observe and describe it in culture, but one part of how we describe it is the idea that it's natural for children to outlive their parents. If you die before them, you leave them to die alone. One mentor tried to convince me once that suicide was intrinsically tragic, that it was not value-neutral. That person, and many others who love me, didn't want me to die. One thing cis people like to lecture trans people about is how transition involves loss. Your parents are going through a loss, other cis parents tell me. Do you feel in pain because you are losing the male part of yourself?

my mother asks me. The Dalai says that when your greatest student betrays you, they become your greatest teacher.** Could this be true of parents and children as well? Maybe this is how I should understand my mother's feelings about my transition, both of us feeling betrayed, both of us having something to learn.

I always think of my father as flexible. He tells me that before he met my mom, he lived in a tiny apartment with a tatami mat, one plate, one bowl, one pot, a pile of books and only a few pairs of clothes that he had sewn himself, though he was a university professor at the time and could have afforded many more indulgences. Standing in my parents' sprawling house full of my mother's things—medical journals, photographs she's taken of the family, her plants, the furniture she's collected from yard sales and estate sales, tapestries and paintings and etchings she's bought at junk shops and public markets and from her friends' artist children, as well as more banal tchotchkes, like a tiny figurine of the Queen of England, or a little headless action figure that was a toy of mine from my childhood, leaning against the soap dish on the window sill above the kitchen sink—my father murmurs to me, "I never thought I would live in a house full of so much stuff, I would never have liked it, but it doesn't really bother me. If it was up to me I'd probably get rid of a lot of it, all this, all the shit–" he gestures around the kitchen– "but it's home. It's nice."

My mother held onto everything, kept track of everything, struggles to give things away. When I was a kid, one of my chores, occasionally, was to go into the basement and put issues of medical journals from 25 years ago into boxes and haul them up the stairs and then out to the end of the driveway for the recycling to pick up. As I was boxing them up she would come interrupt me and tell me which issues of a given journal not to throw away, which ones she wanted to leave stacked in the basement, because they had some article of interest, or something one of her friends wrote. She has my long hair in an envelope from when I cut it myself as an eight-year-old, she has every costume I ever wore, every painting or drawing I ever made. She stores some of these things in my childhood room, as though I'm the one keeping them. She lives in a museum of the life of the family, of her own tactile and imaginative connection to the family life she manifested out of creativity and her own adolescent loneliness, and her sheer will. She doesn't want to get rid of things because it's comforting for her to have them around, because they make her reality real, even if they degrade the quality of the space, attract dust, require constant sorting. Even broken things, even discarded things, she doesn't want to get rid of them yet.

I'm like her, it's hard for me to throw stuff away. With friendships, even if I don't talk to someone for years, even if someone wrongs me, or harms me, I always try to be open to them. I'm a glutton with material things as well. I have plastic ziploc bags full of headphone splitters, HDMI adapters, picture-hanging nails, tubs full of nail polish remover and cotton swabs even though I never do my own nails, bins under my bed full of speaker wire and machine parts, and of course every letter that my mom ever sent me. Someone once told me this impulse to hoarding was about Jewish intergenerational trauma. I look at my stuff scattered around my messy bedroom (cleaning it takes three days in this phase, so hard to remember what I'm doing on so much k) and I think about my anger at my mother and my father's seeming resignation about her collections of stuff. When I first came out to her and she was very upset, he told me that she was having a harder time with my transition than he was, but that she would "come around." When I call them on the phone today, they're cleaning out the basement, "so you don't have to do it when we die," they say. Some part of them understands that the work they don't finish in this lifetime will be mine to continue.

[i made this meme when i couldn't get out of bed; the bechdel test is a feminist thing about movies, that's like "is there more than one woman character, do they talk to each other, do they talk about something besides men," i think..]

pt. viii, trans girl suicide museum 4: humiliation (early spring '18)

The lived experience of transphobia for this girl—largely because of the protections afforded me in white supremacy and class oppression—is not one of constant overt aggression; instead, I mostly just experience pervasive minor humiliation. Not to say that I haven't been assaulted or followed or screamed at or harassed or all the shit. Just that I'm a white girl, that I could get access to money even if I didn't work for a while, I can navigate complex medical and social service bureaucracies—and get treated in relation to my whiteness in said bureaucracies—and I can relocate to be near trans communities, trans friends, and other kinds of things I need in a way that's impossible for many of my sisters. This discrepancy in itself has a tinge of humiliation in it, but is also an indisputable blessing. That said, it's kind of a shitty blessing, in that it cuts me off from being relatable in certain ways to other trans femme people, and is predicated on there being people who don't have the same access to safety and resources. This is one way that class operates as a system, by giving people options that alienate and isolate them from communities, and then pitting them against those communities. This is part of the structure of gentrification, of expensive education, of class mobility. You identify with the thing that gives you power (e.g. having a fancy education) and then like a virus it poisons you, shrivels your ability to connect and be real with most people.

The feeling that my class privilege has alienates me from other trans girls has motivated me to hide it or lie about it, and pretend I'm chill and broke and one of the group. I don't think I fool anyone though, and also I think it's pathetic and creepy when people who have money lie about it and try to hide it, like the white people pretending not to be racist in *Get Out* or something. Lately I have just been trying to be as real as possible about it, even though it's uncomfortable and sad to do so. I imagine a life where I work to move resources (wealth, land, power, safety) to sisters of mine who live with the daily threat of violence, assault, eviction, incarceration. Once I get out of this part of the museum I will go harder, I tell myself, once I can get out of bed and not be high and feel something besides acute distress.

I'm about to travel to see my family and can't stop thinking about what I'm going to wear and how I'm going to dress, about my cis mother and cis sister, and how they deeply believe I'm a man, and how if I get anything wrong, like need help with my clothes, or attract to much attention with my makeup, or do anything that doesn't feel authentic to them, or anything that feels too masculine to them, or anything like that at all, how I'll be so humiliated, because I won't even be doing a good job of my charade, I won't even be a convincing fake. That's one of the things I whisper to myself when I feel horrible in public: "you're not fooling anyone."

Another thing that's humiliating is feeling crazy, like being psycho all the time. Before I went on hormones I was excited to go crazy and I don't know what to say about it now except it's working, I cry every day and am addicted to ketamine and my Juul and sometimes can't get out of bed or do any sequential task.

Is the idea that one would need to deteriorate or get broken down in order to be liberated? My dad asked me, "if transitioning is supposed to be about finding your true identity and coming into yourself, then why are you and all your friends so down in the dumps?" Transness should be purely freeing and happy, says the mainstream gay-pride-respectability-assimilation story. "The idea that queerness is about discovering your personal truth and therein being healed is part of a capitalist conspiracy that centers personal identity over solidarity or collective power or broader cultural and societal justice movements," I blurt out at my father. I'm not sure he's totally following.

I come out to a friend of mine from college, Michael. In college we watched dozens and dozens of movies together, and today we just went to see a movie in San Francisco, and then are eating sushi in Oakland, before Hazel picks me up. I am wearing a full face of makeup with a giant blond slick ponytail on the top of my head and an oversized white t-shirt says "THE DAYS OF THIS SOCIETY IS NUMBERED" that Cyrus gave to Claudia, and Claudia gave to me, and I think is an art thing but I don't know what it's from. This is how I dressed to meet Michael, a cis straight guy who nonetheless has a faggoty affect and sensitive aesthetic sensibility.

Right before Hazel picked me up I told Michael I was transitioning, that I was on hormones. He was so sweet about it, so moved. He said he had noticed how I was dressed and my makeup and thought something might be up. He asked if he could give me a hug. And he said he thought it was one of the most courageous things a person could do. This struck me as an insight. When I posted a meme about getting told I was beautiful by cis women strangers in public, and how it reminded me that I just wasn't passing, several girls commented saying that their fatness often got them the fake praise of being "brave," as though a normal person would simply not be fat, or hide their fatness by never leaving the house. But Michael telling me I was courageous felt loving, maybe because he was not a stranger, maybe because he had known me for years, since I was 17, and had watched me drift through different relationships and styles of dress and other social and emotional commitments (are there other ones besides relationships and clothes? IDK) and he somehow had some info about what it would mean for me. Michael is a very sweet and effete man, who can also be very cynical, so I imagined his saying I was courageous coupled with his knowing me for so long had some hint of cynical realism, or some awareness of a bizarre reality that I struggle to comprehend: I could have not transitioned, that I transitioned not because it was inevitable, but because I'm brave. This is not to say that being trans is only a choice, or that people who don't come out are cowards, or any other transphobic lie you might read in my interpretation of Michael's observation. He was simply noting, I think, that it takes a certain kind of fearlessness to approach the totem of one's assigned gender and say "despite the fact that I shall not be rewarded for what I am about to I do, I will desecrate this shrine such that only weird people will think I'm sexy forever."

This observation of courage has helped me, especially as I confront my deteriorating mental health. My understanding that I am both getting better and worse, that I am moving towards something that I deeply want, and that the road inevitably leads to—and only maybe through—the museum, well, this understanding is one I try to hold for myself the way a parent might hold an infant: loving, protective, forgiving. This is what I wished for from my parents, and also why I could never say to them the depth of the museum in detail, why I had to try to keep a game face. They already didn't want me to be trans, who would want their kid to be a fucking mess the way I am now. Like a stunted version of my teenage self forever.

I keep thinking about an essay I wrote for a psychodynamics course in my organizational theory grad school where I made an analogy between Kleinian splitting and balancing the way that oppressed people are both noble for their suffering and also just having a shitty time. I wrote this essay when I was fully closeted, a trimmed-beard-J-Press-trench-coat-and-Odin-blazer-Hickey-Freeman-pressed-shirt young professional closeted trans girl working at a consulting firm studying organizational psychology at the graduate level at a fancy university, and trying to be a do-gooder. What follows is an excerpt from that essay:

I was in a workshop about disability justice led by a disabled activist. She named that growing up with a different body than the people around her, there were two dominant narratives available to her. One was the narrative of disability, that she was less than and worse off than people who were able-bodied. (In tropes of U.S. antiblack racism, this narrative's analogue might be the image of the black child trapped in the ghetto, deprived by poverty and unable to escape or ascend classes.) The other was what she described as the "super crip" narrative, of disabled people overcoming adversity and achieving "just the same" as able-bodied people, a kind of rose-colored picture that ignores or downplays difference (in racism, this narrative might be embodied by mainstream black celebrities like President Obama who strove for excellence in various white institutions, and were ultimately successful).

This binary, or splitting, between total disempowerment or total equality, also has the quality of Kleinian splitting. Either being non-white, non-male, non-straight, is just worse and bad, or it is "diverse" and wonderful and unproblematic. The trainer in the disability justice workshop described a third path of understanding, the "social justice" path, that admitted of complexity. I have overcome adversity and thrived, the trainer said, and I have also suffered ... The pique of sadness linked to the deepening of love and realization of complexity with which Melanie Klein characterizes the depressive condition may also be a fruitful way of understanding the developmental arc of adults coming into awareness about the realities of social injustice.

A continual struggle for social justice movement organizations will be balancing the aim to empower all people and specifically historically disempowered people, while also avoiding the kind of combativeness, defensiveness, and splitting, that are endemic to all extreme ideologies but cause specific harm in radical left spaces that at a high level are striving for healing and transformation.

In turn, a struggle for mainstream organizations (where the dominant discourse of the business community is of terse, clear explanations with clean emotional edges) will be to tolerate the deep complexity of identity issues and historical disempowerment, and openly engage the varied emotions that come up for people, both empowered and disempowered, around acknowledging identity and training staff in understanding identity issues.

I wish I could say this to all my classmates at grad school. I wish I could show them the videos I send Hazel of myself rolling around the floor of my room blaring unlistenable electronic music, wrapped only in the most delicate lingerie, completely out of my body on k. I think about my friends who have survived sexual assault and how they have these certain kinds of insights that other people don't. I think about my friends who live with chronic illness, who have spent their 20s knowing deeply what it's like to be close to death. I think about myself crying in the women's bathroom stall silently, waiting for the group of women who just entered to leave, so no one sees me.

These two split narratives, the "oppressed people are just worse off" narrative and the "oppressed people are superheroes" narrative, have a specific shape and flavor with different oppressions. Transphobia tells a number of bizarre stories about transness and trans identity. I'm about to try to write about a crazy thing that happened to me but I'm scared and I'm crying as I write, and maybe that makes it make more sense for a reader to know that.

Last year I joined a Re-evaluation Counseling group in West Philadelphia. For the uninitiated, Re-evaluation Counseling (RC) is a peer-to-peer liberation therapy framework (invented in the 50s and popularized in the following decades, I think). RC counselors believe that we are hurt in critical ways as children that then get logged as global "distress patterns" in our adult lives. These distress patterns make us do irrational things, like believe that when our lover is angry at us, it's the same as when our abusive parent was angry at us. This theory is not significantly different than many other mainstream psychological theories.

What's kind of interesting about RC is what they believe about healing, which is that in order to transform our distress patterns, we need to "discharge" our painful emotions. Discharge is a physiological process. You can do it in five ways, by laughing, crying, shaking, yawning, and maybe yelling (-I think, I can't remember exactly what all the rules are). RC sessions are designed to provoke discharge, usually by the counselor offering "contradictions" to our distress narratives. So if my distress loop says I'm unlovable, a counselor might tell me "you deserve so much love, no matter what you did wrong, you deserve all the love," and as you might imagine, hearing this contradiction as I'm talking about my unlovability could be very emotional, and so I would cry and cry, and in doing so, supposedly move through my distress. Or maybe I would laugh and laugh. Or roll around on the floor and shake. It's somatic and forgiving.

RC has been described as a cult, and I sometimes felt like it was a cult, especially when people were laughing to discharge. We would sit in a circle and an older, experienced counselor would talk about something that was painful for her (her dying mother, the election, her sexual trauma) and she would laugh and shake uncontrollably, deep echoing laughter that seemed to make her mouth and throat and eyes and the veins in her ancient hands all bulge to cartoonish size; in these moments, sometimes, I would feel that my classmates were acting like deranged people, cackling about their pain. Witnessing people discharge often felt extremely strange, and also, in good moments, extremely sacred. The task of a skillful counselor is to hold the complexity of someone's distress, regardless of what manner of discharge was presenting. A person might be screaming and crying and then switch to laughing, or they might be mad at someone else and then switch to being mad at themselves. The job of the counselor is to see what the deep underlying distress message is, underneath the signals on the surface. I found the early phases of learning about these practices to be nourishing and insightful.

My preferred method of discharge was weeping. I would cry about how adults got angry with me when I was a kid, about how I was not sure I deserved love, about how my exes thought I was a bad person. After a really good session, I felt like I had been rinsed off, like my bitter and sour emotions had been power-washed out of my nooks and crannies, and my sense of hopefulness and personal meaning had been renewed.

I'm not really concerned with whether RC is a cult, partly because I think the anxiety about cults in white U.S. mainstream culture is symptomatic of a cultural suspicion of anything that asks too much of the individual, anything that's not a nuclear family or a nuclear war that asks for sacrifice must be wrong. (What's more, I suspect that Americans' doofy susceptibility to cults seem like it's born out of this same suspicion actually, like we don't have good criteria for assessing if a charismatic leader is going to fuck us over.. but this is an aside). It is, however, worth mentioning that the founder of RC is somewhat of a cult figure; a tiny photo portrait of him hung above my RC teacher's bed, though the founder was long dead. The founder was also accused by a handful of women of sexual abuse and sexual harassment, of course in the name helping them discharge their distress. There's a huge archive of writing about people's experience with this stuff on the internet, of which I've only read a little bit.

The founder believed that homosexuality (and of course, therein, transness) was part of a distress loop from childhood trauma, and that sufficient discharge would help queer people have "rational," "healthy" cis hetero adult lives. This is important because RC also names sexism and racism and classism as explicit ills, so there was a tension in early groups between an emphasis on liberation and social justice, and on the other hand, deep homophobia.

As I understand it, in the 80s and 90s, gay people who had been exposed to RC methods had fought fiercely within the organization to shift the narrative, to say that gayness was not in fact a trauma response but a defensible identity, and that gay people did not need to be converted out of their gayness. Trans people, at least at some levels of the organization (which is an international network) have not been so successful.

When I entered RC, I was asked about my use of "they/them" pronouns. At that point I was still a cis-passing guy, not yet using the name Hannah, and not yet on hormones. My hair was almost shoulder length, in delicate waves, and I dressed like most of my friends in west philly at the same, in soft, worn clothes, usually tight jeans and an old t-shirt. I was non-binary identified, but still a 'guy' to other people in many spaces. I was told in my first meeting with the course leader that trans people were not allowed in RC. "It may seem oppressive, but it's not," she explained. We were sitting in her large kitchen on a tree-lined street south of Baltimore avenue, copies of *Mother Jones* and *Utne Reader* strewn on the table, along with the day's newspaper and some mail. "We've been told by the international reference person on trans issues in our organization that we're not equipped at this point to support trans people around their mental health." This explanation confused me slightly. Trans people were being prohibited from participating in RC in order to protect them. The teacher then asked if I was trans.

I really wanted to learn about RC (several of my friends were very invested in it) and it seemed OK to enter into a space where I was not going to be witnessed in all of my gendered nuance. I needed therapy badly, and I thought this might be a good alternative. It was $120 for twelve classes, or $10 for a class every week. After that, I would be connected to a network of peer counselors who I could counsel with for free whenever I wanted. It seemed like a good deal.

I told her I wasn't trans. I used "they/them" pronouns because I have a complicated relationship to my masculinity that I was interested in working on in RC. Right answer. I was allowed into the class.

Over the course of the next nine months, I was taught how to be counseled, how to counsel. Several times I was put in a group with cis men where we had to talk about the ways that sexism hurt and dehumanized us, the way toxic masculinity had shut down our emotions and sensitivities, and made us into tough guys. This narrative didn't fit my experience and I grew to dread these moments.

I started hormones during the course sequence. My friend and roommate who was also in the course (a gay cis girl) asked me at some point: "are you going to be OK not talking about trans stuff in your counseling sessions? It's a huge part of what you're working on right now." I laughed and said I'd be fine, that I had lots of problems I needed counseling about. I began wearing makeup everyday, which at first I would wash off before class. By the end I was showing up with a full face and a gel manicure. I still tried to wear masc clothes, but I often do I guess (thinking about Sophia's comment about my white jeans and navy baseball shirt). My friends were freaked out and upset by me hiding my transness in the class, they experienced it as an indignity I was facing.

When the course ended, there was a month-long hiatus, and we were asked if we wanted to join another a second course, an advanced course. I didn't understand that this was part of the deal, that the coursework went on ad infinitum. At this point I had come out as trans in a number of significant situations, including to the M's parents and Elizabeth's parents. I was trying to figure out how to come out to my parents. I had started telling my close friends to call me Hannah. It felt bad to think that I would opt into a space where I would still have to be closeted. My hair was longer now, and I was getting my eyebrows done every two weeks. I was getting the hair lasered off my face. Even when I wasn't wearing makeup, I looked like something was up with my gender. I was less and less cis-passing.

I arranged a meeting with my teacher. Perhaps we could work something out. I didn't have a clear goal. I went to her house in the afternoon and we sat on an orange couch under a labor union poster in the room where I would have counseling sessions. I stuttered through my coming out speech. I don't remember exactly how I opened but it involved a confession that I had been thinking a lot about my gender and that I was identifying as trans and what would this mean for my place in RC. My teacher seemed very perturbed. In a grim tone she responded that this may be an obstacle for me continuing to engage in RC. She explained, once again, that this was not because of a bias against trans people, but because trans people were not able to be fully supported by RC leaders in the current regime. "It may resemble oppression or exclusion," she re-stated, "but it's not."

I responded with the courage maybe Michael was imagining. "To be clear," I said "when privileged people make decisions on behalf of marginalized people, I believe that's oppression. If you wanted to empower trans people, you would give them all the information, and then let them decide. You wouldn't decide unilaterally that it wasn't a good fit and then bar them from entry or kick them out." At this my teacher suddenly back-pedaled. "We're not kicking you out. You can stay in the class. I just want you to know that it may be difficult." She paused. "When we first met," she told me, "we discussed how in RC, every part of your life may be held up for examination. This would be no exception. So if you're prepared for that.." she trailed off.

I thought I understood what she was saying, but wasn't sure. I started in the same way, again "To be clear, it sounds like what you're saying is that my trans identity would be held up as a potential delusion or illness, to be unpacked, and healed, so I can live my life as a man?" She paused. "Well," she was speaking carefully, "that may be what the founders of Re-evaluation Counseling believed. That's not what I'm saying. I'm just saying that every part of your life has to be available to be held up for examination."

I went for it. "Re-evaluation Counseling teaches that different oppressions affect people differently," I began. "One part of how transphobia works is that trans people get told that being trans isn't real, that we're not really trans. In this way it's different than other oppressions. Women are told that sexism isn't real, but they aren't told that they're not women. Black people are told that racism isn't real, but no one disputes that blackness exists. But trans people are told, as part of trans oppression, that transness isn't real, that the identity we claim is a delusion. So if that's one of the underlying assumptions in this community, it would be hard for me to be in this space. I'd love an opportunity to hold my transness up for examination," I went on, "but it might be unsafe for me if the people I'm in the space with are assuming that it's a mental illness to be gotten rid of by discharging my emotions and then living my life as a cis man."

There was silence. The teacher then did something so deplorable that, even given everything that had already happened, I was even surprised. She named that she, a white lady, might not have a problem with my transition, but that other members of our course were older African-Americans who had grown up in Christian traditions, and were probably homophobic and transphobic. She used more veiled language than this of course; she said they may not be tolerant, she warned. She avoided naming her own transphobia and blamed the people of color she was supposedly collaborating with and teaching with. The kind of thing white people do when they're alone with each other all the time. I was stunned. I had been able to defend trans people moments ago, why couldn't I call out this blatant racism? Maybe I had just run out of steam. I said nothing. I told her that I would think about it, and she said she would also think about it. I asked her if we could counsel 1:1 if I wasn't in the class. I didn't want to get fully cut out. Probably I'll have my hands full doing 1:1s with people who are enrolled in the class, she said. I left her house.

A day or two later, I received this email:

It was good to see you and think together about your questions about RC on Wednesday. I did have a good talk with my regional reference person after that. We could see different ways of looking at the issue, but as we talked we both got clearer that it doesn't make sense for you to be in the class. As a community we don't have the resources to offer the amount or strength of experienced counseling that we would wish to, and it wouldn't be right to agree to continue and offer anything less. I am sorry that this is where we are right now, and especially sorry not to have regular contact with you. I do care about you and wish you well as you continue on your journey.

The story remained the same, that the organization did not "have the resources." In a way this made sense to me, as a social justice educator who had met the rage of the people of color frustrated with being invited to participate in white-dominated spaces. The RC leaders didn't want to invite trans people into a place that would be bad for them. At the same time, I didn't believe that people with dominant identities should gatekeep their spaces; they should give marginalized people all the information, including information about the potential risks and disappointments, and then let those people decide. I felt that I should get to decide, not them. Her letter braided into a familiar thread in the history of anti-integration rhetoric, whether it was letting women take on responsibility in companies or letting POC into universities— "it's for their own good to keep them out," the argument goes.

My friends were upset, and my roommate quit RC. A leader in an RC chapter in another city contacted me to talk. I didn't want to deal. Dealing with cis people's ire about this injustice was too much for me, and I told them it was fine, I was fine. The reality was that the humiliation was severe.

For a while I've felt like people tearing their hair out over TERFs was weird. Why would I want to be included in a cis women space? RC was not a women's only space, but certainly saw itself as a feminist space, and certainly didn't see excluding me as an act of violence against women. But why, my line of thinking goes, would I want to be included in a space that didn't want me?

Last night, in Oakland, Jamie brought me to Essex, a Japanese-style hot tub for women only, in someone's backyard, that anyone can enter for free if they have a keycode to unlock the gate. The space is all silent and unbelievably dark. The tub is extremely hot and after you sit in it for a bit, you can go lay out on one of several wooden platforms nested among pine trees, naked under the stars in a backyard in a city. Last night there was someone else using the tub when we were there and I was so worried that she would feel freaked out that I was there, that a non-cis-women was in the space. Even though there's graffiti in the shower area that says "Trans Girls Siempre" and has a heart drawn around it, I had no idea if it was chill for me to be in that space.

I thought in that moment about my TERF position, my "why bother with TERFs" argument. It was premised on the resilience of trans girls, that we could get what we need from other spaces if we were not allowed in cis-women spaces, in TERF spaces. I know that believing this for me was in part born out of my class privilege, my sense is that I could leave and go somewhere else if I couldn't be treated as a woman in a given space. I know that lots of trans girls don't have this material mobility, as well as my sense of entitlement, my sense that I deserve to get what I want. Part of my class-based mobility was the ability to cast scorn on those who excluded me. But thinking about this at Essex, and feeling so relieved when the other woman there smiled at me, a big smile, a "don't worry sweetie, I'm not a TERF smile," as though she had noticed me hiding my body from her, I realized that part of what I was avoiding in my feelings about getting kicked out of RC, part of why I dismissed complaints about TERFs, was just the plain humiliation of being trans and experiencing transphobia, the humiliation of the way that transphobia, like I explained to my RC teacher, functions as a kind of sociocultural gaslighting (you don't exist, they tell us, you simply are wrong), the humiliation of not having a legal or medical system that can integrate you. One of my friends tells me they don't want to change their legal sex because they think that their insurance would not cover illnesses pertaining to organs that they're not supposed to have. I don't even know if this is true, but it's scary. You get to choose between being a guy on your driver's license or getting to have a pap smear covered. Or whatever the case may be. Like so many white women before me, I had moments of wanting to distance myself from other women's struggles, a distancing enabled in part my material advantages. But part of how being trans helped radicalize me was that the humiliation of admitting my own privilege and the way it has distorted my sense of reality is no longer the scariest or most humiliating thing.

On top of this, the humiliation of being crazy. The humiliation of being told you're crazy and then also being actually crazy. Just thinking about it makes me want to do k and lie down. In my grad school class, as an introduction, we're asked to say what the most important thing we've done in our lives. Everyone in the class, *literally everyone*, all twelve people, say that getting married was the most important thing. I want to say getting out of bed this morning. I want to say doing k with Hazel at a club in Queens last weekend when we locked ourselves in the single user bathroom and peered at each other through either side of the legs of a chair that was in the corner, curled up on the floor, each of us, saying how much our friendship was a monument, how we helped each other survive, blowing ketamine off of her cellphone and texting Rovena and telling her to come to the club. R came and we did more k and then all went back to Hazel's house and talked about this cis girl Hazel is dating who has only dated guys, and how it feels fucked up to Hazel sometimes, like she's worried that the girl relates to Hazel as a guy, or relates to their relationship as a "safe"—rather than a real—queer relationship because Hazel has a penis. R got upset and was like "that's wrong," and then Hazel got upset and we all did more k and held each other, I wanted to tell my classmates that that was the most important thing I had done in my life, and then walk out of the room. I can't even remember what I actually said, maybe getting arrested at a protest. Being asked the most important thing I've done in my life in a room full of cis people. That is humiliating.

I tell a trans friend that cis girls used to want to fuck me, and now they have no idea what to do with my body, are afraid to touch my penis. "Of course they're afraid," my friend says, "your body is haunted."

[i think i made this right after going through TSA in a weird outfit and then getting intensely searched and non-consensually touched, and wondering if i should've just done a normal outfit, and then being like 'no bitch, you do you']

pt. ix, trans girl suicide museum 5: neutral zone (late spring '18)

I am at Mardis Gras and somehow am flying to New York tomorrow to do an interview at another graduate school, a doctoral program. I'm extremely high, on a cocktail of MDMA, ketamine (obviously), LSD, and maybe alcohol? I can't totally remember. I was walking with Ross, and he was telling me about his transition, about the years when he started hormones and got top surgery. He tells me he was so befuddled, that he didn't know where to go or how to be. He told me he spent part of that time fucking people as a cold top, not letting them touch him. Later, he said, he couldn't even touch other people. In that time, he said he really wanted professional validation, felt preoccupied with his career.

We are sitting on the steps of some friends' house in New Orleans and I can't stop crying. My Juul has run out of batteries so I'm smoking his American Spirits and coming down from like five drugs and feeling the pain of not knowing my future, if I will be a dumb trap with a shopping addiction who can't act regular forever. Ross tells me that so many things changed for him, and while they were changing he really didn't know what it was going to be like at the end, where he was going to wind up. I feel this pain now, the ambiguity of the museum, not just not knowing if I'll ever escape, but if I did, where I would even be, would I even want that life, do I even need to stay alive to see what happens at the end of the movie.

I had a particular experience of double resonance recently, re-telling Ross's narrative to a new friend. I was sitting in my car at 4am in greenpoint with this new friend who I met because they messaged me on instagram (an extremely efficient and beautiful way to meet other trans people) and they were teling me about their transition, about how they might break up with their girlfriend because she said she didn't want them to turn into a man, and I told them about what Ross said about his process and how deep it was—the withdrawal from sex, the refusal to be touched, the fear of professional failure, the deep confusion—and they burst into tears.

Hearing that Ross wanted professional validation filled me with dread because I also want it so bad, want to be in those spaces and be validated, maybe because it makes me feel like my parents will love me, maybe because it makes me feel like I will be legible to random people on the street, even if they want to scream at me or attack me when they figure out I have a dick, maybe it will make me more than just another random trans girl, sad and disposable.

At the same time, I have always felt extremely fucked up in professional spaces and I'm not totally sure why, probably in part for reasons related to gender and being closeted, but there's some other part too. There's this organizational theorist who's popular at my grad school, Edgar Schein**, and in a few of his books he talks about this idea that there are four relational levels in society. The first is—1: exploitation, no relationship, or negative relationship– and he gives the example of prisoners, criminals and people from other cultures; just generally relationships where people dehumanize each other because of oppression (he doesn't say it like this, nor does he acknowledge the way that, say, most of my friends dehumanize cops because we all fucking hate cops).

The next level is 1, acknowledgement, civility, transactional role relations. He gives examples of people we see on the street or people in "helping" roles like servers at restaurants. Here again he doesn't acknowledge the exploitation that people in helping roles often face (e.g. servers getting sexually harassed and having to roll with it if they want to be tipped).

Level 2 is recognition as a unique person, a working relationship. He gives examples of co-workers, people in working relationships, clients or subordinates. He says these relationships require a baseline of trust, like that people in these kinds of relationships generally are expected to be reliable and not withhold information related to their work tasks. Again, here he doesn't acknowledge exploitation in these situations, how they are often defined by mistrust, nor acknowledge the way sometimes people's most extreme emotions can come out towards their bosses, subordinates, or other co-workers.

Level 3 is the trippy one, "Strong emotions—Close friendships, Love and Intimacy." He says that this kind of relationship is generally undesirable in work situations, because people expect active support from people in these relationships in a way that bosses can't usually give. Level three is like the one that twists me up and pulls me, the one that makes all my shit come out.

academic white dude social relationship taxonomy

Level -1	Openly violent, dehumanized relationships	e.g. "criminals," foreign militants, the subaltern
Level 1	Civil, transactional, public relationships	e.g. server at a restaurant, uber driver
Level 2	Recognition as unique person, working relationships	e.g. co-worker, acquaintance
Level 3	"Strong emotions, close friends, love and intimacy"	e.g. kin, besties, partners

[here's a visual I made of his annoying categories which nonetheless helped me in my thinking]

I think one thing that's so intense for me in professional spaces is the alienation of level 2, that is, of level 3 being prohibited. It may not be a coincidence, with that in mind, that two of my most significant romantic relationships in my life were born out of level 2 relationships in level 2 contexts, one with my college professor and the other with my co-worker and boss. I think level 2 relationships scare me in part because I am obsessed with level 3 relationships, feel so defined by level 3s, (should I start referring to my closest friends as my level 3's?) don't have a sense of myself in a concrete way that's extrapolated from level 3. And because the only kind of level 3 you're allowed to talk about in level 2 spaces is your husband, i haven't always known how to explain myself to my friends in level 2 spaces. Sometimes, when I describe my best friends when in normie (i.e. level 2) spaces, I get asked if I'm secretly in love with my best friends. Romantic supremacy and heteropatriarchy are such that having an alternative kinship structure where your primary relationships are desexualized best friendships is, like, illegible.

I hate this hierarchy Schein draws partly because it's normalizing alienation. People who love each other shouldn't collaborate and be productive, he says. I can't remember which dude in Plato's *Symposium*** gives a speech about how the most powerful army would be the army of lovers, because they would fight so hard to protect each other and want to look hot and brave in front of each other. This resonates with me, like if I was fighting in an army with Cyrus I would want to be as brave and beautiful as possible.

Maybe that is a helpful way of thinking of my friendships with other trans people. We are fighting together to survive.

There's also just something really emotional for me about the alienation of level 2 spaces, the way they feel for me specifically, and I think that has tortured me most of my life any time I've had to be in one. I wonder if it will be different after my transition cements more, if I will feel more at peace in alienated workplaces, or if I will still be tearing at the boundaries, trying to get them to go away, or just receding, doing the least and trying to disappear. My therapist asks me why I'm addicted to drugs and partying. I want to just say that they're suicide adjacent, that when I'm really high and deep in the music, I almost don't exist. Instead I tell him that boundaries go away so fast in those spaces, that you get to be really connected right away. He asks me what else it is about it.

I think I feel obsessed with being witnessed, and maybe there are limitations to how witnessed you can be in a level 2 space. I feel allergic to alienation. And this new alienation of being flattened, being seen as nothing more than a dumb girl, a dumb trap, an overeducated annoying white trap, a man in a dress, a predatory man who can't get an erection, a man in Shaina Mote overalls and an Ulla Johnson jacket that Hazel bought me, etc. etc.

The day after me and Ross's talk after Mardis Gras where I cried on the sidewalk, I go to a grad school interview in New York, but another thing happened first. I flew into Philly and drove to New York, planning to spend the night at Hazel's apartment before my interview. My body is fully detonated and turned to ash from partying for literal days, staying up 'till 4am then getting up at 8am to go to parades, taking more drugs, covering my face and body in different shimmering paints and fabrics. This Mardis Gras felt good because almost all my costumes were clothes I just normally wear sometimes. Clare wrote on her twitter in 2013, halloween feels redundant when everyday I put on my woman costume, and I felt that during Mardis Gras. I'm already a druggy slutty zombie, but this week everyone else is on my level.

Anyways I get to Hazel's house back in New York after returning from NOLA totally obliterated and am letting myself in (I have a key) and she is for some reason in bed with her ex and her ex's new girlfriend and they are in the middle of some business. I have an interview the next day at 11am. I get into bed with them. I kiss Hazel pinning her arms above her head and biting her nipples. Good baby, she whispers. I am rolling around with her ex's new girlfriend, we are locked at the mouth, touching each others' tits and backs and stomachs and flanks. I can't totally remember what happened, but I remember kissing Hazel so tenderly, feeling her body under mine. Somehow I make it to the interview the next day, with a full face of perfect makeup on, head-to-toe Issey, perfume on my neck and wrists, and clever answers to all of the boilerplate questions. I'm astonished that I can walk.

A few weeks later I get into the grad school. Upon reading the acceptance email, I start clicking around the website and seeing all the courses I will have to take, I feel fear about how unmotivated I feel. I stay up all night with Lena and forget to take my hormones and then have a fight with Hazel about her not visiting me enough. I stay up all night with Beth and Rooni and Coco do blow and go to the doctor and call Claudia on the phone a lot. I want winter to be over and it's not, I want to feel that it's safe or chill for me to be in a romantic relationship but it's not, I want to feel surrounded by loving and supportive friends but I also don't want to get out of bed.

One of the last books assigned to me in organizational psychology grad school was called *Managing Transitions*, which is about organizational change, not being trans. It's weird though, because when I read it, it just made me cry and cry. The book is about this idea that when something changes, there's this ethereal aura around the actual change, the emotional halo of change, called the transition. (To be clear, the author does not use the phrase "ethereal aura" and certainly not "emotional halo"). He does, however, describe something very bizarre and haunting, which he calls the neutral zone, the liminal area between the old way of doing things and the new way, the area after change has begun but before it has reached its actualized new state. He says the neutral zone is often defined by the feeling of loss that's experienced during a transition.

I weep while reading this because it occurs to me that he is talking about the suicide museum, he's talking about what Ross described, when Ross said that there are so many things that are going to change and after which you'll feel different and you still don't even know what all the things are. The author of the transitions book says that navigating the neutral zone is about emotional competency around loss, that when corporate leaders initiate change, they usually fail to acknowledge what personnel are going to lose. This makes me think about my own feelings of loss, and the way others have tuned into it.

My mom asks me about this, in a way that feels insidious. Why are you sad now? she asks. Are you mourning some loss? I think she wants me to say that I miss being a man, that I regret transitioning. That's what it feels like. I lay into her in a weird way. I tell her about men staring at me on the street, about getting assaulted late at night on the street in my neighborhood, about hiding in the stall of the women's bathroom, trembling.

I talk about people staring at the picture on my driver's license from five years ago and raising their eyebrows, about being humiliated when I'm shopping for clothes or buying make up, about getting touched by random men in public and at parties, about being terrified to be pulled over by a cop while driving or have any interaction with police officers, about how I think like no one wants to fuck me and if they do it's because they're fetishizing me. She gets really sad. This is what the neutral zone is about for me, about losing whatever was good about being read as a white man and cis, namely some kinds of conditional safety, permission to be left alone. Even as I'm writing about this, I feel disgusting and stupid for trying to explain it, annoyed that I feel misunderstood by my mom. I get on the phone with Cyrus, and we talk about our writing projects, about hating what we're saying about trans experience because it's all changing so fast. When we finish writing can we just leave, Cyrus asks, can we just take a trip and leave and not come back.

The grad program I'm finishing is intolerable, a toxic level 2 space. I had a call with a professor yesterday—she is the first person in my program who I've come out to. The professor asks about my transition. It's good I say. I saw Caitlyn Jenner in a restaurant in California, she tells me. Wow, I say. He held the bathroom door for me, for the women's bathroom, she says. Gosh, I say. His hands and feet are so big, she says. Yeah, I say. He was an incredible athlete, she says. Yes, I say. His, I mean um her body is huge, my professor tells me.

Yeah it's really interesting to see people in public and see the different choices they make about their bodies, I say calmly. Well I just wanted to tell you that story because I thought of you, my professor says.

I tell my mom about this interaction and my mom says my professor isn't so much transphobic as transignorant. I don't put up a fight. I'm bored of putting up a fight. My mom tells me there's an article about FFS in the New Yorker. I can't remember the name of the surgeon, she says. I start naming surgeons. Yes, that one, she says.

I'm exhausted of being a trap. My penis is a different shape. My breasts are a different shape. I wonder if my face is changing shape. I had sex a few times—and thought for about a week I was in love—with someone in New York. Then I suddenly felt disgusted with myself and with them, I felt like we were too obsessed with each other, and I felt fetishized, and disgusted by my own sexuality and my own desire, and by being desired. I abruptly cut it off, to their surprise and sadness. Then I felt like a monster again, an exterminating angel. I experience hopelessness about romance. I experience hopelessness about sex. I wonder if I will ever have a positive sex experience again.

My professor, my Caitlyn Jenner professor, asks if I've come out to anyone in my grad school cohort. I tell her no. I feel like I have to but I don't want to. But I tell her I will. She says she hasn't told anyone. Her job, besides teaching classes about organizational development at Penn, is working as a consultant, mostly to pharma companies. She has to keep a lot of secrets, she reminds me as we're talking. I think of myself as a big house with many rooms in it, she says. There are things behind one door and then I close that door, and there's a different room, she tells me. I think this image is beautiful, but I'm annoyed at her. "Like compartmentalizing?" I ask. Yes, she says. Your secret is safe with me, she says. I decide to come out to my class, partly because I suspect like it will build credibility with this professor even though I don't want to be close to her. Power is weird like that I guess. Here is the draft the letter I write them:

Hi all,

I wanted to write to you about something big that's been happening in my life in the past few years.

I'm in the process of a gender transition; I'm using the name Hannah, and she/her/hers pronouns. I've been on hormone replacement therapy for over a year and am in the midst of a number of medical procedures, including permanent hair removal on my face, and currently planning to undergo facial feminization surgery this fall.

I've felt nervous about talking about this in the cohort space for a number of reasons, partly because it's been an intense and vulnerable process, and also because I wasn't sure how it would be received. I've generally been hesitant to talk about it with people who didn't already know, and if I've dropped off communications or been hard to get a hold of, this has been why. I still appreciate the time and learning we all had together, even though I've needed some space from it.

I hope all is well with all of you.

best, Hannah

I wrote a paragraph in the letter about how if people had 101 questions about trans issues or trans women's experiences, to just google them, but then I took it out. My feet are strapped in really tight, the trash is piled really high, I'm really really wandering around the museum. I have so much aggression towards this particular group of people, these arbiters of the last cis space I had to go into all the time as a closeted person, these normie normal people with their weddings and/or marriages, their straight cis kids (or their closeted kids) and how I would dress like a man long after I was comfortable doing so in order to avoid dealing with this, to avoid coming out to them. It's funny that I told them I was getting surgery, I felt like I had to so they would know what I meant by being trans. Cis people don't get it unless you're getting cut open, I deeply feel this.

There was one day in class when my classmates were talking about an adult learning exercise they'd done in another class, where a student had to demonstrate teaching something to the group. One woman had taught a man how to apply mascara. How hard can it be one of my male classmates wondered out loud. It's complicated! a female classmate asserted, explaining that there were certain things men just didn't understand or know about. I felt the feeling of being illegible, dripping, creppy, horrifying, unimaginable to them. None of you know anything about me, I thought. The meme of the guy standing in the corner at the party complaining, except the guy is a trap and she's saying "do any of these cis normie business school grad students even know what it's like to go home and just lie on the floor totally dissociating on K"

When I changed my pronouns, I didn't tell anyone in my grad school. But at that point, because almost all my friends were queer, and I worked at a coffee shop where people were good about pronouns (a bunch of trans and non-binary people worked there) grad school was the only space where I was consistently misgendered. At that point I was using 'they' pronouns and identifying as non-binary in most spaces, but when I heard someone in a grad class use 'he' pronouns for me (ew I shudder) I would whisper to myself, as an act of defiance, "I'm a girl." I would say it multiple times a day, a tiny prayer, an assertion of my deep gender over the gender they were reflecting back to me, a tiny amplification of the dissonance. It was not a plan I made, it was a reflex. Fuck you. I'm a girl.

The explicit course of study in my program was about organizational development, and therein how groups and teams worked. It was particularly painful for me because even as we discussed unconscious group assumptions and norms, I was silent about the intensity of the cissexism of the group, the straightness of the group, the corporatism of the group, the normalness of the group. Our conversations were ornamented with peculiar architectural features of capitalism, ugly logics that made no sense. People believed what CEOs said in their books about how they turned around companies, never discussing the ways that these books are marketing ploys which are often inaccurate, and very rarely acknowledge workers' experiences, especially low-level. People believed that CEOs opinions about political issues mattered. People followed the sales and mergers of companies the way many Americans follow sports. People thought it was generally good to be wealthy, people liked cops, people thought it was good to be well-spoken, good to be powerful. One woman was kind of obsessed with sexism in the workplace, but her idol was Cheryl Sandberg. I think this classmate was aware of my transition, partly because she was obsessed with women and femininity and would notice things like my nails and eyebrows even before I came out to her, and I also think she might have known because I had told her about my meme account. She mentioned transwomen in the workplace to me, once, in passing, but maybe also just because she knew I was an SJW, because all my presentations were about diversity and inclusion and identity and emotions at work. I never even got my classmates to a critique of identity politics because they were barely aware of identities to begin with, besides man/woman.

I'm on an airplane flying to Florida a day after my last class of grad school yesterday. I got so fucked up last night, mixing coke and K and drinking probably a fluid cup and a half of tequila over the course of the night, make up still smeared on my face, reeking of the cigarettes that were being smoked at the drag show, being smoked at the illegal sex party in the church basement, being smoked in Coco's bed where Rooni and Coco and Hazel laid on top of me, cuddling me while we watched rap videos until five in the morning, after the church party was shut down by cops. One of my classmates asked me how I was going to celebrate my last class of grad school. I said I was going to go out. I can barely hold my head up, hungover and on 3 hours of sleep, but furiously typing. I guess I need to talk about this.

pt. x, TGSM 1,000: *The suicide museum refers to a specific transness, and that transness has a specific shape*

when you are really in the struggle for liberation from gender oppression but you're low-key worried that the norm of asking people to introduce their pronouns along with their name contributes to a culture where even non normative gender is supposed to be legible, definable, controllable, and ultimately regulated by the same power structures you're trying to resist, as demonstrated by the expectation that people be "out" and "proud" about their gender queerness or gender subversion in order to have legitimacy or authenticity in their identity

[this is one of the first memes I made, when I still felt like I shouldn't even post memes because of my male privilege]

"Whatever the opinion of biologists on this point, the idea that there exist complex, obscure, and essential relationships between sex and truth is to be found—at least in a diffused state—not only in psychiatry, psychoanalysis, and psychology, but also in current opinion."

Foucault, *Herculine Barbin*

One scary part about coming out to my business school classmates—or really any normie people, any people who have never thought about or dealt with trans identity—was knowing that whatever I said was going to get interpreted and scrutinized based on their pre-existing idea of transness. It's also true that them getting to see me as a trans person probably changed their ideas of transness, maybe changed their lives, their senses of their gender in general, simply because none of them had ever chilled with a trans person before, seemingly. This is what I would tell myself when I felt disgusting and afraid sitting in class. You're changing their whole lives, I would say to myself, you're giving them a gift. It still felt horrible to be near them.

There are these teenagers I get into arguments with on the internet who identify as "Truscum." If you already know about truscum, you can skip this paragraph where I explain it. Truscum are trans kids who believe that transness is a binary medical condition defined by dysphoria. They believe that "real" trans people experience dysphoria as defined accurately by contemporary psychiatric professionals and represented in the DSM, and that anyone who doesn't experience this specific condition is trying to capitalize on transness; they refer to such people trying to capitalize as "transtrenders." Truscum I have seen engage in a lot of cyberbullying, often telling other teens who identify as non-binary or who don't look 'trans enough' that they're faking. They hold up stories of "transtrenders" who start hormones and then stop and detransition, because they felt dysphoric when their bodies changed. Truscum caution that it 'ruins peoples' lives' if people start hormones and then want to stop.

There are a number of things that are irritating about Truscum. One is that they're mostly trans boys under the age of 18. They seem mainly motivated by their desire to assert their personal authentic transness, often in opposition to other cis-passing teenagers who identify as trans, usually on tumblr, but sometimes at their middle or high schools. They do not seem interested in a broader agenda of gender liberation, or of transness as troubling or disrupting dominant gender norms. Rather, they assert that true trans people have a medical-biological issue that requires them to medically 'switch' to the only other 'opposite' gender. Trans people want to be cis people, they argue. Transness is not an identity or a political position, they argue. Being trans is not fun and interesting, they say, it's a medical condition. They don't have a critique of white supremacy, or modern medical discourse, or trans experiences before medical transition was normalized in the last 20 years. It's like none of them have read Foucault.

I get hung up on Truscum because I experience an intense double-reaction to their extremist rhetoric. On the one hand I find it to be extremely fucked up, shallow, and destructive. On the other hand, as a binary trans bitch, I find their seriousness about transness and their irritation with cis-passing non-binary people with septum piercings and asymmetrical haircuts who are really into announcing their gender variance to be extremely relatable. Some of the queer friends who really supported me early on in my transition were such cis-passing non-binary people, who touted their transness in activist spaces but who didn't care about using the bathroom of their assigned gender, didn't bother coming out to their families (and in fact often had placid relationships with their families who had no idea that they used "they/them" pronouns) and never navigated the horror show wing of the museum that is medical transition (e.g. hormones, surgery, etc.). I actually love and respect a lot of these people, and the generosity and openness with which they met my transition is part of why I am where I am today. At the same time, I think I ultimately had to distance myself from many of them, when I realized that there was an implicit false equivalency between their annoyance with gender as a set of roles and my deep desire to have a differently gendered body, to have a different life. And this is a Truscum refrain: it's fine to want to get rid of gender roles, anyone should get to act and dress however they want, but not liking gender roles doesn't make you trans.

And the other reason I feel attracted to Truscum comes back to the private symbol thing I was writing about so many months ago I can barely remember but is important again here. Like, some SJW trans lib people sometimes say that having a penis shouldn't be a symbol of maleness, that my penis shouldn't make me feel like a boy ("some chicks have dicks"). But also sometimes it does make me feel like a boy, so then I just feel like I have false consciousness or internalized transphobia or something, for having dysphoria. I think there's this SJW idea that if I was liberated I wouldn't need to change my body at all. And there's something comforting about the conservatism of Truscum, of being like, "look, if your body feels fucked up, that's what being trans is," and it makes me feel relaxed, sometimes, to be like "yeah I'm not a bad trans girl if I cried when my FFS appointment got approved by insurance because I was so happy, I don't need to be an enlightened trap who knows I'm a girl even if I never pass." Because I want to pass, even though the idea of passing is fucked. And I want to validate trans girls and trans women and trans feminine people who don't feel that they need to get surgery or don't want to change their bodies, but I also want to validate myself, and we're all walking wounds hungry for validation over here in the suicide museum. Like maybe if everyone got infinite validation somehow, how many problems that would solve.

When I was in New Orleans during Mardis Gras—this same most recent time with Ross—I was gliding through the night in an acid-ketamine chariot when I encountered Laura, who described herself as "a masculine person," wearing an iridescent white wig and fully unzipped white jumpsuit with her top surgery scars visible, beating people up on the sidewalk. More specifically, Laura was hitting people in the face as they requested it, while holding fourth on her technique—and really philosophy—of slapping and hitting as part of queer sexual discourse. I approached and asked her to hit me. I liked it so much that I asked her to do it again and again and I dropped my beer bottle on the ground and glass flew everywhere and someone yelled at us and Laura yelled back at them and we laughed and then walked around the corner and sat down on the sidewalk and I laid in her lap and we blew k and talked about Truscum.

Laura, it turns out, was a queer theory professor, and when I went off about Truscum (seriously I was so high I have no idea why I was talking about this) she responded in kind. It's intense, she said, my students, (referring to her undergraduates) there are some that are so into being publicly genderqueer, publicly experimenting, calling people out from the rooftops, etc. I worry, she says, about the shy quiet kids in my classes, the ones who feel to me like nascent gender freaks, who may be trans and closeted, that there won't be room for them, that they won't want to join the asymmetrical haircut / septum piercing parade. In some ways I resonated with the shy kids Laura was talking about. I didn't want to be out and trans in college because the queer kids seemed shrill.

But I don't want to blame shrill SJW college queers for anything, because they're doing the same thing Truscum are doing (and the same thing I'm doing in the museum) however distastefully, which is just trying to navigate a culture that tells us personal identity matters a lot, consumer identity matters a lot. A huge part of my experience of affluent white American culture, since my childhood, was being expected to define myself as an individual, through my dress and taste and academic performance and literally any other choice I made. Like making a character at the beginning of an RPG. Public symbols as everything, starter pack meme as everything. And I think this context of constructed self-hood in alienated consumerism is conducive to anxiety, and I think young people who are negotiating with queerness and transness sometimes want those variances—especially since they're punishable with the painful consequences of homophobia or transphobia—to do a bunch of work for them. A lot of young people—and I struggled with this too— want queerness or transness to answer the existential question, "who am I," when in fact the construction of that question in alienated consumer capitalism is basically unanswerable in a meaningful personal way.

And herein is my most pressing philosophical problem with Truscum (besides that non-binary identity is real and valid, that transness is a process and destransition isn't a failure, and that Truscum are literally often just being shitty adolescent bullies). The deep problem for me is their assertion that transness is a stable category, one that can be cleanly demarcated with medical diagnosis, and cleanly treated.

A bunch of sections before I talked about the Metzl book about the social construction of schizophrenia.** If you don't remember, the gist of the book is about how schizophrenia was believed, in the early 20th century, to be a disease afflicting primarily middle class white women, whose symptoms were framed around delusions and introversion creating an inability to, like, reliably perform housework. It was not a violent or threatening condition. Later, with the rise of the black liberation movement, the diagnosis came to primarily land on politicized men of color, was associated with aggression and paranoia, and served as a justification for hospitalization and incarceration.

The idea that was a hinge for me before is the same idea I want to come back to now: Metzl says that it doesn't make sense to talk about schizophrenia in the middle ages, since the category didn't exist in the same way as it does now. Whatever we believe and describe about schizophrenia in the 21st century is so particularly defined by our culture and times, that even if the symptoms clustered in similar ways at a past time, the contemporary experience of it, the cultural category, the diagnosis, would be unrecognizable. The idea of illness, the idea of the individual, the idea of sanity, are all part of our time, and not translatable easily to other moments in history, other times.

This idea profoundly affected my thinking about my transition. There are all these particular assumptions and norms in our culture that are prerequisites for understanding and describing transness. Being trans is often getting told to us as a medical story, but it's a story of our particular time and culture, not some cosmic truth. To use the example I was just talking about, part of the reality of contemporary transness that's different now compared to 150 years ago has to do with a contemporary cultural expectation that young people define themselves as individuals and consumers as part of their process of coming into adulthood.

It's not that I don't participate in any socially contingent beliefs about transness. Like, I actually do believe in my spiritual connection to a legacy of gender variant people (in part because of the emotions I felt in my childhood and adolescence reading and hearing about queer and gender variant people in all different contexts). I also believe trans women have always existed in some way, because I can feel it in my body, I can feel a sense of ancestry. This idea of gender-variant time travel is a construction too, of course, but it's one that gives me life.

I also feel like it's important to be careful about mapping contemporary definitions of transness onto historical peoples, partly because it's a. a little boring and b. kind of imperialist. So I don't go around saying "trans women have always experienced themselves as spiritually connected to each other in a legacy." And again, this is what bugs me most about Truscum is that they posit to know the truth about transness, as though such a truth was plain and simple and could be exhibited in a museum that you could take a tour of, and then understand the thing, as though shit won't just keep changing, with trans people learning new truths and ways of being all the time. Part of what this means is that having solidarity with trans people involves not imposing a universal idea of what transness is on anyone, while at the same time also staying suspicious of trans narratives that give power over to cis doctors, cis law makers, cis media moguls (for example, Truscum narratives).

I say all this because I'm haunted by this one idea, what the foucault quote at the beginning of this chapter says, this idea of one's sex being related to one's human truth.

If we lived in a culture where one's sex and one's personal truth weren't seen as twinned, transness would be less of a revelation, less of a big deal. Being trans could be like being a Catholic in secular culture, or being a libertarian in an apolitical culture; that is, it would be an attribute you had, but not necessarily *the* thing about you, a political or spiritual conversion perhaps, but not a referendum on your human truth.

If we lived in a culture that was less homophobic and anxious about homosexual experience, then transness would be less troublesome, since part of what transness does is trouble the assumptions around the construction of homosexuality (e.g. how can I be a dyke if i am fucking someone's vagina with my penis). Or as I said to my mom, "I'm a chick with a dick, so anyone who wants to fuck me is basically gay" (she didn't totally understand). The anxiety around transfeminine desire and interpolation into homosexuality is well captured by the trope of the "trap" in anime: that you get tricked if you thought a girl was hot but then realized she had a dick, because desiring someone with a dick would make you gay, and therein trigger all these problems for your identity.

If we lived in a culture that was less obsessed with embodied desirability, and that didn't so violently value some bodies over others, trans people would probably feel less disgusting.

If we lived in a culture with a higher tolerance for ambiguity, rather than obsession with measurement, fixed identity, and knowability, transition wouldn't be so confounding to people, and the process might be more normal. Epistemologically, we are anal retentive. Not rigorous, just stressed out. We need to know what a trans girl is. What are you, trans people get asked. Where are you from, people of color get asked. White supremacist capitalism wants to make a map of everything, and then monetize the ways that things move around on the map. Basically literally. The museum.

This is part of the reason why I feel weird about introducing pronouns when people meet each other in groups; it creates this expectation that each of our genders should be mapped and appropriately invoked at any time, that I'm safer if someone can say exactly what I am, and that I would be harmed if my gender every confused anyone (or confused me). I'd rather be misgendered than be "accepted" by an establishment that's making some kind of ominous bio/political truth claim about what my transness is. I don't want a trans utopia where there's 200 genders on the census box. I don't want a trans utopia where instagram asks me my pronouns and my sex assigned at birth and then targets marketing at me. I don't want cis people to make money using images of bodies like mine.

Maybe it's just like why k is better when you can't buy it at CVS, because there's some part of transness that cracks or fucks with all these cultural norms I'm talking about, and this current cultural moment of trans visibility is probably actually about securing transness in a sack of amber and declawing it and making it legible (the way gay culture has been ripped from the anonymity of the dark bathhouse and into the stagelighting of the reality show.. lots of people have critiqued this one).

My friend Denise, who I met at a retreat for descendants of holocaust survivors, studies addiction narratives, among other things.** Denise told me this idea that I can't get out of my head and that I think is really beautiful, which is that when we talk about curing addiction in secular culture, it's predicated on this capitalist idea of a self-regulating subject, someone who, if left to their own devices, could control their own behavior and decisions. Denise talked about how indigenous communities where people are more heavily connected to one another and dependent on the community to regulate their bodies and behaviors (rather than being alienated like white and/or capitalist communities and just having do self-regulation) often have different relationships to substances and addiction, but that when those same communities become colonized and people start having more alienated capitalist first-world lives, addiction problems suddenly spring up.

This idea made me think about Austen Riggs, a kind of progressive psychiatric hospital that uses community and interconnection as a technology to help people heal their mental health. At this hospital, there's no locked doors and patients have to consent to their treatments, and everyone in the community talks about their feelings about everything (like, even the janitors) as part of the community maintenance. When I talked to an acquaintance who worked there, I asked him "how do people ever leave? like if the mechanism of healing is the community?" he explained that leaving the hospital is an extreme trauma for some people, and many relocate to other kinds of intentional communities.

What does this have to do with transness? I guess I was supposed to figure out that I was trans alone– which if it's not yet clear, I didn't, a lot of other people helped me. But the idea is that I was supposed to have self-insight and then do self-exposition, and then make these different individual plans (like planning surgery on my individual body) to make my transness real. But what if my transness hadn't emerged in a context where we believe that people are self-regulating subjects? What if a community had unlocked my transness? What if instead of discovering my own transness inside of me, I could say G-d discovered it, that the G-d wanted me to be trans? Or that I had it passed down to me from an ancestor? Or that I was living a truth and struggle that was manifested in me by the community of all transwomen forever?

Earlier I said one definition of transphobia could be the dissonance between how a trans person feels, and how they're treated, plus violence. As I piece together all these elements of transness as a category constructed in our culture, I am starting to feel this feeling that transphobia, too, is part of the construction. We've diagnosed transphobia to be getting misgendered, so we start having gender diversity trainings at people's workplaces. We can't yet diagnose transphobia as there being police at all, and needing to get rid of cops and prisons to get rid of transphobia, so that's not how it's defined.

I'm sitting in a Korean bath house in Tampa where I passively allowed staff to think I was a man in order to gain admittance. This is supposedly bad for me, in a mainstream trans-liberation framework. It's supposed to cancel my identity if I have to say I'm a man to go to the bath house. But I don't feel bad right now actually, and I think that's important.

At first I was nervous; the cis lady at the desk called me sir a few times, and I was nervous to step into the men's locker room, as I have been my entire life; I remember being at the YWCA as a kid and afraid of being teased or pushed or beaten or stripped or called a faggot in the locker room, so those feelings come up for me, even as an adult woman, entering the locker room with my long hair and painted nails and full face of make up, little buds of breast from the estrogen and androgen-blockers, shorn pubic hair. When I undress and walk into the men's naked bathing area, there are only two people, both muscular and with large moustaches and piercings on the round tips of their penises. They are standing in a shower, washing each other. As we make eye contact, they smile at me and nod, and a wave of relief hits me hard. They immediately see what I am. I feel their recognition and their pleasure at my sharing the space with them. I don't need to be asked my pronouns. I don't need to talk about my gender journey. I'm just home with my siblings, and it doesn't have to live in language.

And in this safety, with these men, is where I suddenly felt a coherence around my anger about the ways I've been taught about transphobia. I'm supposed to think it's *really fucked up* that I'm wearing a blue robe and eating my kimchi jjigae and typing this in the gender binary bath house. I know girls get assaulted like this in spaces all the time, and that's part of the issue; we want to protect trans people, so we come up with solutions; but that's the other part of the issue, like how the solutions themselves create new fucked up modes-

-like is the solution to girls getting assaulted in gender binary spaces having cops at the bathhouse? Or not letting girls like me be in rooms with men like those guys at the bathhouse? Do we need to have wings of exhibitions, taxidermied bodies, historical placards, educational videos, guided tours explaining pronouns and body politics and gender versus sex and sex versus sexuality in order to let anyone into the bath house? Are there supposed to be wealthy board members who believe in the mission of the bathhouse, and groups of school children who go gawk at me and these guys in the bathhouse? Do we need gender studies classes to take trips to the bathhouse?

Do we need a docent? What about an unpaid intern? Do we need guards? Probably there should be guards, to make sure no one touches the bodies.

Part of why the museum is fucked is because it's about a kind of knowledge of transness that's about institutional power and social control. Transness in the museum is supposed to make sense, it's supposed to exist in the body and the brain, it's supposed to have medical and legal and neurological places it lives in order for me to be real. But much in the same way that few people feel at home or safe in the DMV, or in an exam room, or filling out a personal identification form at a security checkpoint, the truth of transness that the museum offers hasn't given me life; it's given me anxiety, it's given me self hatred, it's given me fear and resentment and confusion and narcissism and a spiralling sense of lostness, that I'm supposed to want to rectify by making sure that everyone's pronouns are on every name tag and every cop or TSA agent is trans-competent when they pat me down. The particular construction of transphobia we have in mainstream culture prescribes trans liberation by promoting regulation, assimilation, surveillance, control. If misgendering is the problem, then we track and forcibly publicize everyone's pronouns. Then trans people will get relief.

I never felt relief in the museum, not like today, when I can silently and privately cry shrouded in the steam of a sauna of the men's section of a gender-segregated bathhouse, with these other guys in the room with me while I'm crying, knowing that I was both misgendered and deeply seen in my gender on my way in here. That getting misgendered as an offense is predicated on a truth of gendered stability, and even though I have wept and wept and punched walls and bit my lip at the pain of being misgendered, I want to remember what I feel in the steam of the sauna today: that the truth of my transness isn't about having a totally stable, mapped, and controlled gender that never gets bent or blows around or whisps away.

I wish instead of the museum I had gotten to go to a bathhouse, where all the sisters and the mommies and daddies and siblings and gestational and non-gestational parents and elders and babies came to have knowledge together that wasn't knowledge for the state or the police or the doctors or the cops or the administrators, but an other, different one.

A month or so after I first came out to my mom, we were on the phone, wrapping up our conversation. "Alright my boy," she said, and then paused. "Alright my girl," she tried out tentatively. "Alright my boy-girl," she settled on, then paused, adding "this is hard for me." "You get to keep working on it," I told her, trying to sound calm. "We'll see," she said, sounding doubtful to me. I felt so annoyed and disgusted. I sat in my car crying after we got off the phone, trying to figure out what was happening, why it felt so horrible that my mother could not imagine my experience, or my identity, or maybe that she actually was capable of doing so, but was resisting in some ways. Later on, Claudia told me there's this idea in family systems therapy that when something changes in a system, family members make "change back bids" trying to undo whatever is different. When Claudia taught me about this, I recognized the behavior in my mother, over and over. I hadn't learned about that yet though, so I was making up my own ideas.

I was thinking about this idea of imaginative work, that my mother was having to do imaginative work to comprehend me and hold me, that there must be all these different internal pieces of work that she had to do in order to see me and accept me. And of course, see and accept herself, which is this other big challenge, for her and lots of other people. This last bit is important because sometimes it felt like my mother almost took my transition as a criticism of her–how could she not have known, how could she be a good mother and also be surprised by my transition. And I have tried to tell her that it was there, that I showed it to her in different ways, that I wanted her to know over the years, even as she told me that she was happy I was a boy; like literally, once, in my early 20s, when I was trying to talk to her about struggling with my gender and masculinity, she told me she was relieved that I wasn't trans. I knew you loved wearing dresses and that was OK with me, she protests, reminds me lots of parents wouldn't let their son do that. I'm not your son, I say. I haven't told her I'm writing this, I hope right now she never sees it, but probably she will someday, and she will get freaked out that I do too many drugs, and feel criticized about how I describe her, and we'll fight for like three months and then not talk about it again.

Today my pain towards my mother is like a giant statue with a placard that reads "just because transphobia is constructed doesn't mean it's not real."

But she's working in her imagination to do this hard project, and I think that her imaginative work is an act of love towards me that I can see and feel even as I feel tremendous pain about how our process has been in this phase. And her imaginative work is evocative for me too, because it reminds me of the imaginative work that I feel I have to do as a trans person, not to let the museum's knowledge of me or my story be the dominant one. While my mother will work to imagine me as a girl, I will continue to try to imagine the bathhouse, to imagine a way of knowing bodies and gender where no one is forced to be knowable, concrete, connected to truth, etc. Gender as pure private symbol, gender as vapor, gender as the crusted ketamine on the edge of your nose when you wake up in a bed full of other people and can't remember where you are.

And part of what it feels like to me to be around other trans people when we really vibe and get into it with each other is that the whole affair becomes protean, becomes smoggy, becomes disruptive. And as long as it's disruptive, it will continue to try to be regulated, with new diagnoses, new HR policies, new ways of shaming people for being a TERF, new laws to say no one can yell at you for being in the wrong bathroom, when we know as gay people that laws actually have never controlled what people do in bathrooms.

This is not an argument for one legislation or activism over another. It's a wish, one that barely fits into words. It's a group of trans femmes burning down a museum. It's a bathhouse.

Afterword

at one point after a draft of this manuscript was mostly finished i was at a rave and really gone in a k / mdma / poppers / other stuff thing, and elizabeth was dancing behind me and holding me in a hug like i was a little girl and she was my older sister, and i felt this feeling i have felt on k before which is am i exceptional or is everyone the same, is elizabeth and my sacred love the only thing or nothing. and as usual when i get in a binary i have an analytical tool to say, neither thing is totally true or false, and i felt the exceptionalism of everyone at the rave, everyone's uniqueness their stories and bodies and meanings. and i opened my eyes and looked out at the room of heaving humans flashing with sweat in the neon strobe and thick grey artificial fog and i realized that everyone's hearts were beating, whatever drugs were in their different veins were getting pumped up to their brains and the bass was pumping out of speakers that looked like piles of black refrigerators, and the bass pumping and the hearts pumping and everyone could hear the bass and every single person had a pumping heart.

in this moment something catalyzed that was weirder and more concrete—sort of?—, which was like this image of a giant blue molten circle, so big that if you were looking at the center of it, it would be everything you could see, there would be nothing else, mass culture when you're in the center of it, a blue sun, seeing nothing but assimilation. And then there was the answer to my question about exceptionalism, at the very edge of the molten blue-sun-center-of-things, because if i moved where i was looking the central circle was tinged with a fiery electrical edge, tiny explosive sparks, little nodes of invention, creativity, resistance, each person who had chosen to walk on the edge by going to the rave and taking their clothes off and taking the drugs and dancing for hours, maybe not doing violent insurrection, but still participating in a collective that smolders and crackles at the edge of the center-of-things, for process instead of product, just to burn the thing, just to say fuck you, just to feel moments of nondifferentiation, blended consciousness, merging and splitting and cascading.

i didn't and don't believe that raving or partying or getting fucked up in itself is revolutionary or subversive—and i don't think you should believe it either, especially not when streetwear brands or beer companies or anyone else trying to sell stuff to young people says that it is—but I think the thing I felt in that moment was more complex than that. It's the idea that when you trek to the edge of culture, when you go to a freaky misfit space (there were so many trans femme people at the rave) and you really do the damn thing, it's an opportunity to feel how outsiderness isn't just a lonely thing, it's also a collective thing, and that all of the edge-riders, the addicts and the teenagers who snuck in, and the drug dealer people, and the sex-work people, and the actual people who are too crazy to do a desk job, the people too sick to come to the rave, or whose bodies are too sensitive, and the traps and the sluts and the ravers are together in some moments, in oft-invisible tandem, shredding at the edges of the intolerable mainstream. and this sense of collectivism, of existing together to do imaginative non-verbal shared work at the edges of what's possible, it's a little antidote to the loneliness of the suicide museum. i love k because it makes me feel like i'm in a legacy with others, i said that already.

If you don't know anyone who has chosen to have a radical life in a deep way, and you haven't chosen it either, than this may sound like a kind of flat, adolescent "freaks versus jocks" paradigm; and it's OK, you don't have to understand, because you are in the center; you can leave and struggle at the margins whenever you want to. i really believe it's something anyone can opt into if you're willing to search hard and give up certain things, you don't even have to be trans.

but one of the annoying parts of being trans (or a number of other marginalized identities) is that you don't get to choose exactly. i think lots of trans people and marginalized people struggle in a deliberate effort to slide towards the center in certain ways, for safety, or survival, or just because they actually want to be normal, because normalcy too can be a way of healing. and that is OK too. it's just that for me sliding to the edge helped me get out of the museum, or imagine a world where i was not controlled / haunted / defined by the museum, and i think that freedom has meant so much, that spaciousness has meant everything to me.

I guess if you're reading this and you feel yourself to be in the center, especially if you're cis and you have money, i believe that you should give your resources to a broke trans girl. and if you're reading this and you're haunted by the museum too, i hope something in this makes you feel less alone and more grounded, and maybe even more excited about the magic you're doing by even being alive today, and i hope that you're getting to come up with your own stories or convictions or truths, even if it's different than what I feel or believe. If you ever want to get in touch, just DM me, instagram.com/male-fragility

HB

New York City, Spring 2019

References / Notes

pt. i

The video referred to is Riley Dennis's "Can Having Genital Preferences for Dating Mean You're Anti-Trans?" from Everyday Feminism, posted on April 21, 2017. http://everydayfeminism.com/2017/04/cissexist-say-never-date-trans/

pt. ii

This quote comes what I believe is a 1971 Dutch television interview with Foucault, you can search "The Lost Interview," on youtube, or type this in: https://www.youtube.com/watch?v=qzoOhhh4aJg

Mira Bellwether—*Fucking Trans Women* Zine, I think you can just find it by googling.

In the book of Exodus, Moses has his brother Aaron go with him to try and convince the Pharaoh to free the Jews from bondage.

Herculine Barbin is a memoir by an actual intersex person in the nineteenth century in France that Foucault wrote an introduction for; I read it for the first time while I was writing this and it really helped me.

pt. ii.5

The Boy Who Wanted a Baby is a book by Wendy Lichtman published by the Feminist Press in 1982 that is *actually* a kids book about an AMAB child imagining he could get pregnant, which I read over and over as a child _( )_/

Trans-sister Radio: A Novel is by Chris Bohjalian and was published by Harmony Books in 2000.

pt. iii

The phrase "the limits of what you can tolerate" refers to an idea from *Radical Acceptance* by Tara Brach where she says "The boundary to what we can accept is the boundary to our freedom." I have found this idea very helpful for understanding how oppression (which makes conditions unacceptable) messes with people's interior or spiritual freedoms.

Pippi Kessler—"Lessons for Anti-Trump Activists," published on *Medium*, https://medium.com/@PippiKessler/lessons-for-anti-trump-activists-from-act-up-7963 74fb96c

The Protest Psychosis: How Schizophrenia Became a Black Disease by Jonathan Metzl really influenced how I was able to understand some abstract ideas about medical categories and history in really concrete terms. If you don't feel like reading a whole book (I didn't even read the whole book) there's a really nice one hour interview with the author and activist Will Hall at this link: https://www.youtube.com/watch?v=bPC8ZKqY9eI

History of Sexuality volume 1 is by Michel Foucault and has been published a bunch of different times.

pt. iv

This Nietzsche aphorism is from *Beyond Good and Evil*, translated by Walter Kaufman and published by Vintage books in 1989.

pt. vi

Suzanne Kessler and Wendy McKenna, "Toward a Theory of Gender," in *The Transgender Studies Reader* published by Routledge in 2006. The research in this article is totally incredible and if you can't find it let me know and I will send you a .pdf.

pt. vii

The idea that when your greatest student betrays you, he becomes your greatest teacher is from *The Essential Dalai Lama: His Important Teachings* edited by Rajiv Mehrotra, and published by Penguin in 2006.

pt. ix

The organizational theorist here is Edgar Schein and he talks about this idea in the book *Organizational Culture* which has had a few different editions.

This idea comes from Phaedrus's speech at the beginning of Plato's *Symposium*, a "dialogue" or set of speeches about love.

William Bridges wrote *Managing Transitions: Making the Most of Change* which was published by Nicholas Brealey Publishers in 1995.

pt. x

Again, *The Protest Psychosis* is the Jonathan Metzl book discussed in the notes for pt. iii, above

Denise Grollmus just told me all the ideas that I wrote about here, but if you google her you can find more of her writing, she is amazing.